PLAYS AROUND THE YEAR

More Than 20 Thematic Plays for the Classroom

SCHOLASTIC
PROFESSIONAL BOOKS

New York • Toronto • London • Auckland • Sydney

The editors wish to express appreciation to all of the talented playwrights who contributed to this collection. An extra big thank you to Mary Beth Spann, Carol Pugliano, Jane Conteh-Morgan, Sydney Wright, Jaime Lucero, and Lauren Leon for their creative input.

Compiled and edited by Liza Schafer and Mary Beth Spann
Cover and interior illustration by Jane Conteh-Morgan
Interior design by Sydney Wright

ISBN 0-590-49475-9

CONTENTS

Introduction

Welcome to *Plays Around the Year!* Plays are a wonderful vehicle for learning, and this book offers you a whole year's worth of creative dramatics to try with your class. By including these plays in your curriculum, you automatically:

- foster literacy and appreciation for the play as an art form,
- help children understand plot development through dialogue,
- freshen familiar monthly themes,
- commemorate important events throughout the school year,
- build a sense of community in your classroom,
- offer students experience in performing for an audience,
- encourage children to be attentive members of an audience,
- teach children how to be appreciative of other's efforts,
- instill students with a love of the theater, and
- have fun together!

About This Book

This play-a-month book is a collection of 21 plays designed to complement themes and celebrations ordinarily commemorated in the elementary classroom. Because the plays are clearly linked to days and dates featured in the months of the school year, it's tempting to just stick to this suggestion, for example doing the October plays in October and the March plays in March. But each play actually encompasses many different themes and can be enjoyed whenever the time is right for you and your students. For example, the October play "The Ugly Pumpkin" may be used to compliment a science lesson on plant growth or a focus on diversity as easily as it would round out a Halloween celebration.

Following each play is a Teacher's Guide designed to both simplify and enhance your efforts to share the plays in class. In each guide you'll find:

• Background Information—a quick collection of facts to introduce or follow-up the play experience,

• Book Links—a bibliography of theme-related materials to enhance the excitement generated by the play, and

• Extension Activities—cross-curricular ideas to help broaden the play experience.

Ways to Use the Plays

There are lots of ways to share the plays in this book with students. Some require a bit of long-range planning, while others require no preparation at all! Which route you choose—simple or elaborate—is up to you, but here are three basic approaches to consider.

• **Pantomime Play:** With this technique, a narrator reads the whole play for children to act out with movements and motions only. This relieves children of the burden of having to memorize lines and encourages all children to try their hand at acting out a play's story line.

• **Readers' Theater:** In this technique, children are assigned parts in the play to read aloud to each other or to an audience. Students often feel best exploring new characters and experimenting with different voices without the burden of memorizing lines or movements. And even children with experience performing in full-scale play productions can benefit from reading a play aloud with classmates.

• **In-Class Skits:** As students become familiar with plays and the play format, they may want to experiment with acting out scripts for each other in class. As kids become more confident and polished, they may want to invite another class over for an informal performance. There is no need to worry about fancy costumes or scenery at this level.

- **Full-Scale Productions:** Usually most suitable for older children, a full-scale production calls for all the theatrical trimmings: costumes, scenery, props, and student actors willing and able to memorize a script and act it out with stage direction for an audience.

Choosing the Right Play

You know your students' interests and needs best, so you'll probably have a good idea of which plays are right for them. Be certain to include students in the decision-making process; they'll be more enthusiastic about doing a play they hand-picked. As a general rule of thumb, the plays with the least amount of dialogue (especially the two pantomime plays included in this collection) are best suited for younger children. Younger children cannot easily memorize lines and stage directions, or perform a full-scale play production for an audience without an enormous amount of support.

Preparing to Perform

When the time comes to ready students for a full-scale play production, there are ways to prepare without the panic.

- **Read-Throughs:** Conduct several informal read-throughs first. The kids will get used to the rhythm of the script and become familiar with the story. When the curtain rises they will be familiar with the play and where it's headed.

- **Movement Warm-Ups:** As several of the plays in this book incorporate a lot of movement, certain movement exercises can be very helpful before you begin the play process. For example, if a play contains animal movements, do some animals exercises with the whole class. Explore how different animals would move and sound. Have the children "become" the animals in question.

- **Research:** Your students may feel more comfortable with a script if they've researched the topic before doing the play. Tell children that before stepping on the stage, professional actors often conduct long research sessions to acquaint themselves with a character or a time period.

Getting Everyone Involved

Putting on a play is a collaborative effort. Most of the plays in this book are written with enough parts to accommodate any number of students. But what about those plays that do not have enough parts—or enough juicy parts—to go around? One solution is to have several different performance casts. Another is to involve interested children in behind-the-scene action. Students should know that in both professional and amateur theater, there are more jobs than just acting—many talented people work "in the wings" in order to make a production a success.

Children can contribute to the production as:
- Stage Managers
- Costume Designers
- Prop Masters
- Set Designers
- Program Designers
- Ushers

Putting on a Full-Scale Production

Putting on a full-scale production of a play can be both challenging and rewarding. There are many elements that must mesh to ensure your efforts are successful. With a little preplanning and organization, these elements can flow together without a hitch.

- **Casting:** Talk to students about the different roles available. Make sure they understand the responsibility of each.

- **Sets and Props:** Most of the plays in this book are intended to be performed right in your classroom, so the demand for sets and props is minimal. The simple sets and props suggested will enhance the production, but aren't integral to the success of the plays.

- **Promotion:** Have students design posters advertising the performances. Even if your class is putting on a play for another class only, have students design a poster announcing it to the audience. Students can also design and print programs to hand out to audience members before the performance. These programs can include

a synopsis of the play, the names of cast members and production personnel, plus a list of people who deserve special thanks.

- **Parental and Community Involvement:** Play productions are perfect opportunities to develop a connection with the parents and the community. Enlist parents' help in generating costumes, sets, and props. Also collect costumes and props from area businesses. Consider collecting donations at the door and use the proceeds to support a community effort already in progress.

Additional Resources

- *Handbook of Educational Drama and Theatre* by Robert J. Landy (Greenwood Press, 1982)

- *Creative Drama in the Classroom* by Nellie McCaslin (Longman, 1990)

- *Theatre Games for the Classroom—A Teacher's Handbook* by Viola Spolin (Northwestern University Press, 1986)

Rhymes to the Rescue

by Sandra Widener

My name is Liz: Rhymin' is my biz!

Characters:
- Ms. Jordan
- George
- Luis
- Boy 1
- Boy 2
- Amanda
- Nancy
- Liz
- Girl 1
- Other Students

Props:
- lunch items for cafeteria (trays, cups, plates)
- piece of paper
- trophy

ACT 1

Ms. Jordan's classroom, the first day of school.
Everyone is standing at the front of the room, talking.

Ms. Jordan: I see some old friends and some new faces. Let's all say hello to each other. Let's all sit in a circle on the floor.

[Everyone sits in a circle.]

Ms. Jordan: Now I want you to go around and take turns saying your name and one favorite thing you like to do.

Amanda: I'm Amanda, and I like riding my bike.

George: My name is George. I like to play baseball.

Nancy: *[Shyly.]* I'm Nancy, and I like to do gymnastics.

Luis: My name is Luis, and my favorite thing is to play baseball with George.

Ms. Jordan: And next to you, Luis, I see a new student. Tell us your name, please.

Liz: My name is Liz:
       Rhymin' is my biz!

Ms. Jordan: *[A bit startled.]* Rhyming is your 'biz?' What do you mean?

Liz: *[Shrugging.]* I do it all day.
          When do we play?

Ms. Jordan: We'll play later today...er...I mean there's no doubt we'll be going out. *[Shakes head from side to side while smiling.]* Whew! This rhyming stuff catches on fast, Liz! Now let's continue our hellos.

[As the rest of the group pantomimes their introductions, Amanda and George "whisper" together while looking at Liz.]

Amanda: Rhyming's not going to catch on to me. I think Liz is weird.

George: Do you think she's really going to rhyme all day?

Amanda: If she does, I won't sit next to her. I'm not being friends with a weirdo!

ACT 2

Ms. Jordan's classroom, lunchtime of the same day.

Ms. Jordan: *[Helping to dole out lunch orders.]* Liz, did you order pizza for lunch?

Liz: Yes, please!
    With lots of cheese!

Amanda: *[Groaning.]* There she goes again! Liz, can't you stop that?

Liz: But, I like to rhyme
    all the time.

Luis: Can't you just speak like a normal kid?

Liz: *[Shrugging.]* It's no crime
                to speak in rhyme.

Amanda: Come sit with us, Nancy. We'll leave the rhyming girl to herself. ○

Nancy: *[Whispering softly to Amanda while looking over at Liz.]* Aren't we being mean?

Amanda: *[In a loud voice.]* When Liz wants to be normal like us, she can sit with us.

Liz: *[Muttering sadly to herself.]*
    Maybe I don't belong at this school.
    If being me is just not cool!

ACT 3

The classroom, a few days later.

Ms. Jordan: *[Holding a piece of paper.]* Class, I have an announcement. There's going to be a school talent show. Any class that wants to can put on an act for the whole school. A prize will be awarded to the class with the most creative presentation!

Luis: That's great! Let's go for the prize! Now, what can we do to win?

[A few moments of silence.]

Amanda: I can ride my bike and Nancy can do gymnastic tricks!

George: No, it has to be something really different. Besides, we all want a part in the show.

[The kids look around at each other, thinking.]

Nancy: *[Speaking so softly the kids have to lean to hear her.]* Well, I have an idea. It's—no, it wouldn't work.

Luis: What? What?

Nancy: Well, nobody would have anything like it.

Other Students: What? What?

Nancy: Well, what about Liz? She could rhyme!

Luis: Rhyme?

George: Rhyme?

Nancy: Rhyme!

Amanda: How could rhyming be a talent? And how could we be part of that? Not that we'd ever want to, of course!

Nancy: Easy! Liz is great at making up rhymes. We could have kids call out words and Liz could make up a rhyme about each one! Then we could repeat whatever Liz says— we'd be her backup rhymers!

George: Cool!

Luis: Yeah! Let's do it!

Amanda: You know, I hate to admit it, but that *is* a good idea. That is, I mean, if Liz will do it after the way I treated her. *[Everyone looks over at Liz.]*

Liz: A rhyming show?
    I'm ready to go!

Ms. Jordan: Then let's begin—we have a lot of rhymes to fit in! *[Everybody laughs at the teacher's attempts to rhyme.]*

ACT 4

The school auditorium. Ms. Jordan and her class are gathering on the stage. Other students (including Boy 1, Boy 2 and Girl 1) are sitting in the audience.

Ms. Jordan: And now, a big hand for my class who wishes to present their most unusual act: Rhymin' Liz and The Rhyme-Time Kids.
[Applause.]

Ms. Jordan: Audience, just take turns calling out words and Rhymin' Liz will make up an instant rhyme about your word. Then, for your listening pleasure, the Rhyme-Time Kids will repeat Liz's rhyme. Let's begin with that boy over there.

Boy 1: Bat!

Liz: That's an easy one, a rhyme for bat—
        A fat rat sat on fat cat's hat!

Rhyme-Time Kids: That's an easy one, a rhyme for bat—
                A fat rat sat on fat cat's hat!

Ms. Jordan: And now you in the front row.

Girl 1: You'll never get this one: strawberry!

Liz: Just my luck, the Dictionary Fairy
        Granted me a rhyme for the word strawberry!

Rhyme-Time Kids: Just my luck, the Dictionary Fairy
                Granted me a rhyme for the word
                        strawberry!

Ms. Jordan: OK! Now you over there!

Boy 2: Try this, Rhyming Girl: fish stick!

[Everyone in the audience giggles and snickers.]

Liz: *[Taps temple with finger, pretending to be stuck.]* Hmmm.
   A rhyme for fish stick?
   If I only had a wish stick!
[Simulates moving a magic wand through the air.]

Rhyme-Time Kids: A rhyme for fish stick?
                     If I only had a wish stick!

[Kids copy Liz's pretend wand movements.]

Boy 1: She's amazing!

Girl 1: How does she do it?

Boy 2: I don't get it. She seems to have a rhyme for every-thing!

[Later, at the end of the show...]

Boy 2: It's time to award the prize for the best act. The judges agreed that it was a difficult choice—everyone put on a great act. But we also agreed that the winner of this year's trophy is Rhymin' Liz and Rhyme-Time Kids!

[Boy 2 hands a trophy to Liz while the rest of Ms. Jordan's class cheers.]

Amanda: Liz, thanks to you we won! I'm sorry I was mean to you.

Liz: That's alright, that's OK!
I don't like to rhyme *every* day.
Some days I just like to talk in Pig Latin!

Everybody: *[Groaning.]* Oh no! Here we go again!

The End

TEACHER'S GUIDE

Rhymes to the Rescue

My name is Liz:
Rhymin' is my biz!

Background

This play can serve both as an icebreaker to bring a new class together and to introduce the idea of children feeling good about themselves. Several of the following books and activities reinforce the idea that everyone has something valuable to contribute—and that being different can be wonderful!

Book Links

Chrysanthemum by Kevin Henkes (Greenwillow Books, 1991)

Hannah the Hippo by Linda Schwartz (The Learning Works, 1991)

I Like Me by Nancy Carlson (Puffin Books, 1990)

Extension Activities

Rhyme Time

Rhyming is a favorite activity for many children; this game gives them a chance to play with rhymes. Create a list of easy-rhyming words (see starter list below) and write each on a piece of paper. Place the papers into a box or bag. Then divide the class into small groups. Have one child from each group select a word from the container. Then set a timer for one minute during which time each group records all the words they can think of that rhyme with the word they chose. At the end of the minute, have each group share their results. Then, just as the characters did in the play, have each group recite their rhymes for the rest of the class to repeat.

Easy Rhyming Words:

- cat
- door
- me
- find
- fly
- king
- art
- go
- book
- light

Who Are You?

This activity provides a good chance for children to find out more about their classmates. Divide the class into pairs. On the board or on a large piece of chart paper, create a list of information that would be fun to discover about each other such as: most and least favorite foods; hobbies; talents; favorite books; most and least favorite school activity; proudest moments; most dreaded household chore; etc. Have children interview each other and record answers corresponding to the items on the list. Then have the students use the information to write brief descriptive paragraphs about their partners. Read the descriptions to the class and have them guess each student's name from listening to the profile.

A Class Act

Invite students to share personal skills and knowledge with the rest of the class by being the teacher for a little while! Begin by generating a list of possible lesson topics such as storytelling, singing, sharing hobbies and collections, dancing, demonstrating arts and crafts techniques, etc. After helping each interested student to decide on a viable presentation, have them each develop a simple lesson plan including a list of materials and goals for the lesson, as well as a series of steps for the actual presentation. Suggest that students practice their lessons on family members at home. Then set aside a regular time for students to shine in class. (After preparing and presenting their lessons, students will undoubtedly appreciate all the preparation work you put into each one of yours!)

Name Poems

Down the left-hand side of a piece of paper, have students use capital letters to print their names vertically. Then show them how the letters of their names may be used to begin sentences or adjectives describing themselves and their strengths. Some students will need extra encouragement to complete this task as they may not feel comfortable blowing their own horn. If some students continue to be stuck, suggest that a close friend begin their lists for them. Interested students may turn their lists into stories about themselves and their strengths. Poems such as *Broom Balancing* by Kathleen Fraser (from the *Random House Book of Poetry for Children*, 1983) and books such as *Amazing Grace* by Mary Hoffman (Dial, 1991) will help to set a positive I-believe-in-me tone.

Planting Seeds, Spreading Sunshine

by Liza Schafer

Characters:

- Narrator
- John Chapman (Johnny Appleseed)
- Ma
- Pa
- Nellie Nead
- Settlers 1–9 (or more)

Props:

- backdrop painted with apple trees

For Johnny:
- tin-pot hat
- coffee-sack shirt
- tattered pants
- planting stick
- seed bag and seeds

For Settlers:
- rugged pioneer clothing

A farm in Leominster, Massachusetts, 1794.

Narrator: John Chapman was born in Leominster, Massachusetts, in 1774. He grew up on a farm full of apples trees. Johnny liked to pick the shiny red apples. But even more, he loved to plant apple seeds so that new trees would grow. When Johnny was twenty years old, he decided it was time to go west.

Pa: We're going to miss you around here, son—especially at apple pickin' time. You're the best darn tree climber in the family.

Johnny: I'll miss you, too. But I have to go west to Ohio because there are no apple trees there.

Ma: *[Confused.]* But I thought you loved apple trees?

Johnny: I do. That's why I'm going. I want to plant seeds so that all the settlers moving there will have wonderful apple trees like ours.

Ma: *[Handing Johnny a sack.]* Well, here's some food in case you get hungry. Apple fritters, apple butter, applesauce, and a big slice of apple pie.

Johnny: *[Smiling.]* They're all my favorites. How did you know?

Ma: *[With a laugh.]* Just a lucky guess!

Johnny: *[Hugging Ma and Pa.]* Good-bye, Ma! Good-bye, Pa!

Pa: Good-bye, son!

Ma: Take care! You'll always be the apple of my eye.

[Johnny waves and walks off stage.]

ACT 2

The woods of Ohio, a few months later.

Narrator: Johnny walked west for many weeks, seeing nothing but trees, flowers, birds, and animals. At last, he met some settlers who were building a log cabin.

Settler 1: Hello there! What brings you to our neck of the woods?

Johnny: I've come all the way from Massachusetts to give you these apple seeds.

Settler 1: *[Whispering to Settler 2.]* Psst! Get a load of this guy!

Settler 2: That's…errr…kind of you. But we just moved here from New York and are way too busy to bother with your silly apple seeds.

Johnny: They're *not* silly! Just plant one seed today and in a few years you'll have a beautiful apple tree.

Settler 1: So?

Johnny: *So!*…so that means you'll have lots of juicy apples to eat when you're hungry. You'll have a special, shady place to sit when you want to read a good book. And that's not all: You'll be able to climb to the tree's tippy top and wave to your neighbor…when you get a neighbor, that is.

Settler 2: Gee, that *does* sound pretty good, but we don't have any money to give you for the seeds.

Johnny: That's all right. Just plant a seed and I'll be happy. *[Johnny hands them some seeds from his bag.]*

Settler 1: Wow, you're A-OK Mister! What did you say your name was?

Johnny: John Chapman.

Settler 2: John Chapman...mind if we call you Johnny Appleseed?

Johnny: Not at all. Folks may think it's corny, but I think it's positively...apple-y! See you!

Settlers 1 and 2: *[Waving.]* Bye!

[Johnny walks off stage.]

ACT 3

The woods of Ohio, several years later.

Narrator: Year after year, Johnny walked through the Ohio Valley planting apple seeds and giving apple seeds to everyone he met. By now, many settlers knew about this strange and generous man.

[Johnny walks across the land digging tiny holes with his wooden stick and dropping apple seeds into them. After a few moments he crosses paths with some settlers.]

Johnny: *[Handing seeds to Settler 3.]* It's an apple of a morning!

Settler 3: Thanks, Johnny!

Johnny: *[Handing seeds to Settlers 4 and 5.]* An apple a day, keeps the doctor away.

Settlers 4 and 5: Thank you, Johnny!

Johnny: *[Handing seeds to Settler 6.]* Cherries are red and berries are, too. But apples are the best for you!

Settler 6: Awesome! Thanks a lot, Johnny!

Johnny: Greetings, young lady. Have some apples seeds to plant.

Nellie Nead: *[In a mocking tone.]*
 Johnny Appleseed, I've heard of you.
 Planting apple seeds is all you do.
 Sharing seeds in the sun and seeds in the rain.
 I wouldn't be surprised if you had an apple for a *brain!*

Johnny: *[With a laugh.]* An apple for a brain...I like that!

Nellie: *[Snottily.]* And what's with that outfit? Are you on your way to a costume party?

Johnny: *[Examining his clothes.]* Well let's see. I don't spend much time thinking about my duds. But this tin pot here makes a fine hat and it's great for cooking apple dumplings. And this wonderful bag holds lots and lots of apple seeds. Have some! *[He puts some seeds into Nellie's hands.]*

Nellie: *[Pulling her hands away so the seeds fall to the ground.]* I don't want any dopey seeds. What good are they?

Johnny: If you plant some you'll find out. All it takes is care and patience.

Nellie: That's dumb!

Johnny: *[Tipping his tin-pot hat.]* Suit yourself. Bye.

[After Johnny walks off stage, Nellie picks up the seeds and puts them in her pocket.]

ACT 4

The woods of Ohio, 1840.

Narrator: In 1840, Johnny was 66 years old. But his life hadn't changed very much. He still spent his time planting apple seeds and giving apple seeds to all the settlers. Everyone came to love Johnny...even Nellie, who was now a grown woman.

Johnny: *[Hands seeds to Settler 7.]* Nature's most perfect fruit!

Settler 7: *[Giving Johnny a high-five.]* Thank you, Johnny!

Johnny: *[Handing seeds to Settlers 8 and 9.]* Nothing is peachier 'n apples!

Settler 8: Cool!

Settler 9: Thanks, Johnny!

Johnny: *[Handing Nellie some seeds.]* Hello! Have some apple seeds to plant.

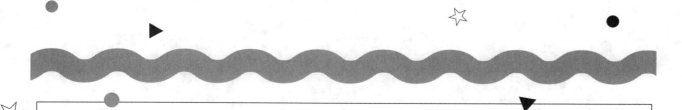

Nellie: Johnny? Johnny Appleseed?

Johnny: That's what they call me. And you are...?

Nellie: You don't remember me?

Johnny: *[Looking closely at Nellie's face.]* Can't say as I do...

Nellie: I'm Nellie Nead. Does this ring a bell?—
Johnny Appleseed, I've heard of you.
Planting apple seeds is all you do.
Sharing seeds in the sun and seeds in the rain.
I wouldn't be surprised if you had an apple for a *brain!*

Johnny: *[Laughing.]* Oh yes, the odd girl who didn't like apples.

Nellie: That's right. I was pretty bratty back then. Is it too late to say I'm sorry...and thank you?

Johnny: *[Surprised.]* Thank you...for what?

Nellie: *[Sweeping arm across the edge of a large field of apple trees.]* For my beautiful apple orchard. After you walked away, I picked up the seeds and decided to plant them. You were right. All it took was care and patience.

Johnny: I'm APPLE-solutely thrilled!

Nellie: Now...how about coming over to my house? I just baked an apple pie and I want you to be the first to try it.

Johnny: I thought something smelled good! Let's go!

The End

TEACHER'S GUIDE

Planting Seeds, Spreading Sunshine

Background

Johnny Appleseed was born John Chapman in Leominster, Massachusetts, in 1774. He grew up on a farm with a large apple orchard. At the age of 20, Johnny strapped a bag of apple seeds to his back and headed west to the Ohio Valley. When he arrived, he began a lifelong mission: going from town to town, planting apple trees, and sharing seeds with the settlers. Sometimes Johnny was repaid with some old clothes or a place to sleep. But more often than not, he received just a thank you. Johnny, who died in 1845, became a nationally known celebrity when a story about his deeds appeared in an 1871 issue of *Harper's* magazine. Since then, many tales have circulated about him including the one that claims he spent a snowy evening snuggled up to a hibernat-ing bear and that he had a special knack for communicating with animals. No one can say for certain how true these stories are, but Johnny Appleseed remains one of America's most popular folk heroes.

Book Links

Johnny Appleseed by Jan Gleiter and Kathleen Thompson (Raintree Publishers, Inc., 1987)

Johnny Appleseed retold by Stephen Kellogg (William Morrow, 1988)

The Story of Johnny Appleseed by LaVere Anderson (Garrard, 1974)

Extension Activities

Sow Some Tall Tales

Tell students that, in the 19th century, lots of folks passed time by making up stories about Johnny Appleseed. Then invite them to do the same. Begin by discussing Johnny as a folk hero. Point out that while Johnny was a real person, people often told exaggerated tales about his life to entertain themselves and others. Brainstorm a list of what-if scenarios with Johnny at the core of each one. For example, what if Johnny befriended a chatty chipmunk or married a women whose passion is peaches? Divide the class into cooperative pairs or groups and challenge each one to develop an idea from the list (or any other idea) into a tall tale. Publish the stories in a Johnny Appleseed Tall Tale Anthology, complete with illustrations. To make your Appleseed Anthology extra special, gather the stories into an oversized apple-tree shape book.

Apple Math

While learning about Johnny Appleseed, the time is ripe to do some real math using real apples. Here are some ideas:

• Place a big basket of apples on a table and challenge students to estimate the number of apples inside. Students can record their guesses on pieces of paper. Then together count the apples to see how many there are. Did anyone come close to the total? If so, invite them to share their estimation strategies with the rest of the class.

• Provide cooperative groups with sets of apples to use as manipulatives. Challenge each group to use them to write one or more apple math problems on a sheet of paper, such as *8 apples – 2 apples = ?*, or *4 apples x 3 apples = ?*, or *1/3 of 9 apples = ?*. Children might also enjoy creating simple story problems. When everyone is finished, students can use their apples to solve the other groups' math problems.

• Bring in several varieties of apples, such as Golden Delicious, Macintosh, Granny Smith, etc. Pass the apples around, asking students to note physical differences among the apple types. Then cut the apples into slices and invite students to taste each one. Discuss which type is the sweetest, the tartest, etc. Have each student vote for their favorite kind. Use this data to create a graph entitled "The Apple of Our Eye." If you like, extend learning by charting the apples' similarities and differences, by baking an apple pie or by sampling other commercially prepared apple products and comparing them to homemade varieties you prepare together in class.

Apple Fest

Celebrate Johnny Appleseed's September 26th birthday with a classroom Apple Fest. Invite students and their parents to contribute samples of their favorite apple recipes such as apple bread, apple pie, apple fritters, peanut-butter-and-apple sandwiches, etc. Label each treat and let students sample. During the Fest, have children make a chart of the top 10 reasons they love apples. Students might also enjoy making apple-head dolls, bobbing for apples, or reading aloud stories about Johnny Appleseed. Cap off the festivities by planting some apple seeds or saplings on school grounds.

Getting to Know You

by Carol Pugliano

Characters:

- Christopher Columbus
- Queen Isabella
- King Ferdinand
- Sailor 1
- Sailor 2
- Sailor 3
- Sailor 4
- Taino Leader
- Taino 1
- Taino 2
- Taino 3
- Taino 4

Props:

- royal thrones (two wooden chairs)
- two crowns
- cape for Columbus (made from a length of fabric or a towel pinned to Columbus's shoulders)
- paper map
- telescope (made from an empty paper-towel tube)
- a beaded necklace
- ears of corn (may be plastic or an empty paper-towel tube painted yellow)

ACT 1

The Royal Palace in Spain, 1492. The king and queen are seated on thrones, wearing their crowns.

Queen Isabella: Well, Mr. Columbus, we've thought about it and have decided that we will grant you permission to go on your voyage!

Columbus: Really? That's great!

King Ferdinand: You seem to be a fine sailor. We look forward to getting all the gold you'll bring back from Asia!

Columbus: I'll do my best to make you proud. Thanks! *[He hurries off.]*

King and Queen: *[Calling after him.]* Good luck!

ACT 2

The shipyard. Columbus is talking with his sailor friends. They are crouched down on the ground examining a map together.

Columbus: Who wants to go on an exciting journey?

Sailor 1: Where?

Columbus: *[Using finger to trace route on map.]* To Asia! To find gold!

Sailor 2: *[Standing up.]* I love gold, but we can't sail to Asia.

Columbus: *[Standing up.]* Why not?

[Rest of the sailors stand up.]

Sailor 2: Well, everybody knows that the Earth is flat. What if we fall off?

All other: *[Muttering to each other and nodding in agreement.]* Yeah! We don't want to fall off! Are you crazy! No way!

Columbus: The Earth is round. We won't fall off. Who wants to go?

Sailor 3: Well...I'll go. I'm not afraid!

Sailor 4: I'll go, too!

Columbus: How about you two?

Sailor 1: I don't know.

Sailor 2: Me neither.

Sailor 3: Come on. It will be exciting. Better than sitting around here all the time!

Sailor 1: Well...OK. Count me in.

Sailor 2: Me too. When do we leave?

Columbus: Our journey will begin tomorrow. I have been given three ships. We'll meet where they are docked. See you then.

Sailor 1: We're leaving tomorrow? Are we crazy? We hardly know this guy!

Sailor 2: Let's take a chance. I want gold!

All others: Yeah! Gold!

ACT 3

Columbus and his sailors are on a ship. Sailors are doing sailing chores—one is steering, another is hoisting a sail, and so on. Columbus is looking through a telescope.

All: Sailing, sailing across the deep blue sea.
　　Sailing, sailing gliding happily.
　　Heave! Ho! Heave! Ho!
　　We're looking for a strange new land to get some
　　　　gold for me!

Sailor 1: I'm getting tired. Is there any sight of land yet?

Columbus: *[Peering through telescope.]* Not yet. I need to get some rest. Let's take turns keeping watch.

Sailor 2: I'll stay up.

Columbus: Thanks. Make sure you wake us if you see anything.

[All but Sailor 2 lay down and sleep. They snore loudly. Sailor 2 looks through the telescope. After a few minutes he shouts.]

Sailor 2: Land Ho!

[All others jump up and cheer.]

Columbus: OK. Let's dock right here. Line up behind me and we'll explore this new land.

[Columbus leads the way as they walk in place behind one another.]

Columbus: It sure is hot!

[All mime being very hot.]

Sailor 1: This beach is very muddy!

[All mime walking through mud.]

Sailor 2: There are so many bushes in the way!

[All mime pushing away bushes.]

Sailor 3: Mosquitoes are biting!

[All brush mosquitoes away from them. These movements are all done while they continue to walk in place in a line.]

[The Tainos enter and move cautiously to the side of the room opposite to where the sailors are facing.]

Sailor 4: I heard something! There's someone here!

Columbus: Where?

Sailor 1: Over there! Look!

[The sailors spot the Tainos. They gasp and duck down. Upon seeing this, the Tainos do the same.]

Sailor 1: What should we do?

Columbus: You stay here. I'll go talk to them.

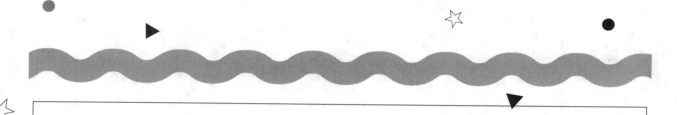

Taino 1: Who are they?

Taino Leader: I will go find out. Wait for me here.

[The leaders rise and approach one another slowly. The remaining members, afraid of being left behind, fall in line behind their leaders.]

Columbus: I am Christopher Columbus. We are sailors from Spain.

[The Tainos look confused.]

Columbus: *[Shouting.]* I said I am Christopher Columbus! We are sailors from Spain!

Taino 2: What is he yelling about?

Taino Leader: I don't know. I don't understand his language. *[To Columbus:]* We are the Tainos. Welcome to our island.

[Columbus and the sailors all look confused.]

Taino 3: I don't think they understand us, either.

Sailor 1: What can we do?

Columbus: I know. Give me some glass beads.

[Sailor 1 reaches into a bag and hands Columbus a necklace.]

Columbus: We want to be friends. Here is a necklace for you.

[The Taino leader takes the necklace, but doesn't know what to do with it.]

Columbus: Here, like this. *[He puts a necklace around his neck.]* You wear it.

[The Taino leader puts it on.]

Taino leader: This stranger is friendly.

Taino 4: What can we give them?

Taino 1: How about some corn. Here.

[He hands an ear of corn to the leader.]

Taino Leader: *[Handing the corn to Columbus.]* You are welcome here. Here is some corn for you.

[Columbus takes the corn and holds it up, turns it around, confused.]

Taino leader: You eat it like this. *[He mimes eating an ear of corn.]*

[Columbus eats the corn.]

Columbus: This is great! Here, try.

[He hands the corn to Sailor 1 who trys it.]

Sailor 1: Wow! I love this! *[He passes it on to the others to try.]*

Sailor 2: Columbus, look. They are wearing gold in their ears. Perhaps they can help us find more gold!

Columbus: Yes, you are right. We will be their friends.

Taino 3: *[To the Taino leader.]* These men are very nice.

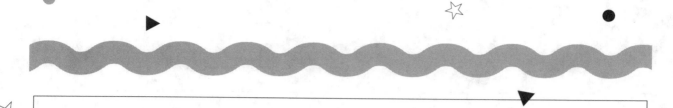

Maybe they can live here with us and help us farm.

Taino Leader: They seem to be good men. Let's have a feast together to celebrate our new friendship.

[The Taino leader motions Columbus and his crew to come with them and mimes eating.]

Taino Leader: Come. We will feast together. We are friends. *[All start to walk off.]*

Sailor 1: I sure hope this works out all right.

Taino 1: I sure hope this works out all right.

The End

TEACHER'S GUIDE

Getting to Know You

Background

Columbus has traditionally been given credit for discovering the Americas. But as many as 40 million people were living in North and South America before Columbus ever arrived.

Queen Isabella and King Ferdinand of Spain agreed to fund Christopher Columbus's voyage to the Indies in exchange for a large percentage of any gold or riches he might find there. Columbus began his journey from Palos, Spain, on August 3, 1492. He was hoping to sail to Asia, or the Indies, in search of gold and spices. After a month-long stop at the Canary Islands, he set out across the Atlantic Ocean. Columbus's ships landed on a Caribbean island on October 12. The Taino (TIE-no) people who lived there called the island Guanahani (gwah-nah-HAH-nee). Columbus called it San Salvador. Since Columbus thought he had reached the Indies, he called the Taino people "Indians."

The Taino were mainly farmers. They grew sweet potatoes, beans, corn, and a root called manioc. At first, the Taino and the Europeans got along well. According to Columbus's journal, the two groups exchanged gifts, and the Tainos held a traditional welcome feast for Columbus and his sailors. But Columbus, in his determination to find gold in order to satisfy the King and Queen of Spain, captured six people and ordered them to bring him to a gold source. Two of the captives escaped. The others led Columbus on a mostly futile search from island to island.

On Columbus's second trip to the Caribbean, he enslaved hundreds of Taino people and put many more to death because they did not find him the gold he wanted. Poor relations resulted in several wars between the Spaniards and the Taino. As a result of these wars, a brutal slave system, and European diseases such as smallpox, the Taino culture was effectively wiped out by 1561.

Book Links

Before Columbus by Muriel Batherman (Houghton Mifflin, 1990)

Columbus Day by Vicki Liestman (Carolrhoda Books, 1991)

In 1492 by Jean Marzollo (Scholastic, 1991)

Encounter by Jane Yolen (Harcourt Brace Jovanovich, 1991)

Morning Girl by Michael Dorris (Hyperion Books for Children, 1992)

The People Shall Continue by Simon Ortiz (Childrens Book Press, 1987)

The Tainos, The People Who Welcomed Columbus by Francine Jacobs (G.P. Putman's Sons, 1992)

Extension Activities

Sing a Song of Sailing

Before reading and performing the play, make a list of the different duties one might perform while sailing. Activities may include: raising the sail, steering the boat, cooking, swabbing the deck, etc. Pantomime these chores while singing about each one to the tune of "This is the Way We Wash Our Clothes" (e.g. "This is the way we raise the sail, raise the sail, raise the sail, This is the way we raise the sail, so early in the morning").

Columbus's Logs

We know so much about Columbus and his voyage because he kept a journal during his journey. Have students imagine that they are crew members on Columbus's journey. Have them keep logs telling what it felt like to travel for weeks without knowing where they were going. Were they afraid, like many people were at that time, of falling off the end of the earth? How did they feel when they first spotted land after so many days at sea? What did they think of the Taino people?

Next, have students write some entries from the Taino point of view. What did they think of the sailors that landed in their home? Were they afraid of them? How did they feel about them living on their island? Did they like it better before or after the sailors arrived?

When all students have had a chance to log several entries representing both sides of the story, have them share their thoughts aloud and then reflect on whether or not Columbus behaved fairly towards the Taino people.

Mapping it Out

On a world map, trace Columbus's first voyage from Spain to the Caribbean. Next, trace the voyage Columbus hoped he would make to the Far East. Compare the two routes and how far away Columbus actually was from where he really

wanted to go. Have children tell of travel tales when they and their families were lost.

Pack and Go

Begin by having the children recount what they packed on long trips they've taken with their families. Then have children pretend they are Columbus and have just received the king and queen's blessing and financial backing for a voyage to the New World. Inform the children that they will be given three ships—*The Pinta, The Nina,* and *The Santa Maria*—and 90 crew members. Have them make an inventory list of supplies needed for a yearlong journey.

The Ugly Pumpkin

by Carol Pugliano

Characters:

- Farmer Smith
- Farmer Jones
- Patty Pumpkin
- Peter Pumpkin
- Paul Pumpkin
- Peggy Pumpkin
- Patrick Pumpkin
- Priscilla Pumpkin
- The Ugly Pumpkin
- Matthew
- Lauren
- Eric
- Olivia
- Kid 1
- Kid 2
- Kid 3
- Teacher

Props:

- six pumpkin shapes (cut from orange oaktag and fitted at the top with lengths of yarn or elastic thread—so children may hang shapes around their necks. One side of each pumpkin is painted with a funny or scary-looking jack-o'-lantern face: the other side is left plain.)
- one yellow squash shape (cut from yellow oaktag, fitted with yarn or string, same as the pumpkins. One side of the squash is painted with a jack-o'-lantern face, the other side is left plain.)
- two paper chef's hats (purchased from a party supply store.)

ACT 1

A pumpkin patch. The pumpkins (plain side out) are seated in two rows of three. They are crouched down as though they are pumpkin sprouts. All the sprouts look the same except for the Ugly Pumpkin, who is a bit off to himself in the patch. Farmer Smith and Farmer Jones enter.

Farmer Smith: The pumpkin sprouts are coming up very nicely this year!

Farmer Jones: Yes they are. I was worried that we did not have enough rain this spring to help them to grow.

Farmer Smith: Well, I don't think you have to worry any more. I am sure we will sell all the pumpkins this year!

Farmer Jones: I hope so. The school is having a jack-o'-lantern contest and I want them to have plenty of good pumpkins for the children to choose from!

Farmer Smith: They will with this crop! *[Farmer Smith stops at the Ugly Pumpkin.]* Hey, this sprout looks a bit odd.

Farmer Jones: You're right. Oh, and I really thought the whole crop was doing so well.

Farmer Smith: Well, let's not worry too much right now. It is too early. Let's wait until growing season and then we'll see.

Farmer Jones: That's right. No sense in jinxing the crop with bad thoughts! Hey, how about some breakfast?

Farmer Smith: You are always thinking about food! Come on inside. I'll make some pancakes.

[They exit.]

[The pumpkins in the patch stretch their arms and rise up onto their knees. They put their arms out in front of them in a circle to resemble a round pumpkin. The Ugly Pumpkin, however, contorts itself into a different shape, not round, but sort of pear shaped.]

Priscilla Pumpkin: Hey! Look at me! I'm a pumpkin! Priscilla Pumpkin!

Peter Pumpkin: We're all pumpkins, silly! I'm Peter.

Peggy Pumpkin: My name is Peggy. Look at my beautiful orange color!

Patrick Pumpkin: Look at how round I am! My name is Patrick.

Patty Pumpkin: I'm Patty and I am a perfect circle!

Paul Pumpkin: I'm Paul, the biggest one here!

[There is silence as all pumpkins turn to look at the Ugly Pumpkin.]

Priscilla Pumpkin: Hey, what's up with that one?

Peter Pumpkin: Yeah. He looks weird!

Peggy Pumpkin: He's shaped like a bell or something!

Patrick Pumpkin: And he's a strange light-yellow color!

Patty Pumpkin: What is he doing here with us? What kind of a pumpkin is he?

Paul Pumpkin: I'll find out. Hey, you! What are you, anyway?

You are the strangest looking pumpkin we have ever seen!

Ugly Pumpkin: Uhh…My name is Samuel.

Paul Pumpkin: Samuel? Even your name is different!

Ugly Pumpkin: I know, I know. I wish I was more like all of you! I'm, I'm, so ugly!

[He bows his head and starts crying.]

Priscilla Pumpkin: There, there. Don't cry.

Peter Pumpkin: Yeah. Take it easy.

Peggy Pumpkin: You're not so bad.

Patrick Pumpkin: Just a little different, that's all.

Ugly Pumpkin: None of the children will ever pick me for the contest!

[He cries again.]

Patty Pumpkin: Shh. I hear voices. It's the kids! Everybody look your best!

[The pumpkins sit up straight and round, and look straight ahead. Ugly Pumpkin does his best to straighten up, but still looks different and wears an unhappy face. The kids enter.]

Matthew: What a great pumpkin patch!

Lauren: There are so many pumpkins!

Eric: I'll never be able to choose!

[They walk among the pumpkins.]

Matthew: Hmmm.... Let's see. I think I'll take this one.

[He "picks up" Priscilla Pumpkin and takes her by the hand and walks off.]

Lauren: This one looks perfect for me!

[She "picks up" Peter Pumpkin and takes him by the hand. They exit.]

Eric: This is mine!

[He takes Peggy Pumpkin and they exit. One by one, the other three children pick their pumpkins and exit, leaving only Olivia and the Ugly Pumpkin.]

Olivia: *[Looking around to see if there are any other pumpkins left.]* I guess I'll take this one.

[The Ugly Pumpkin beams as they start to exit. Matthew enters.]

Matthew: Did you pick your pumpkin?

Olivia: Yes. Here it is.

Matthew: Are you joking? That's the weirdest looking pumpkin I've ever seen! You'll never win the contest with that one! *[He laughs and runs off.]*

Olivia: Oh, I think it's kind of cute. Come on, pumpkin. I'll carve a great face on you and we'll just see who wins!

[They exit. Off stage, students flip oaktag posters over to reveal "carved" jack-o'-lantern faces.]

Teacher: [*Walking in.*] Come on, children. Line up your jack-o'-lanterns so we can begin the judging.

[*All the children enter with their pumpkins. Olivia and the Ugly Pumpkin are last.*]

Teacher: [*Walking down the line.*] Hmmm...very nice. Oh, cute! Interesting! Oooo! Scary! [*She stops at the Ugly Pumpkin:*] Well, well. What have we here?

Matthew: That's Olivia's pumpkin. [*He laughs.*]

Teacher: Well that's not a pumpkin at all. It's a squash! And an adorable one at that!

Kids and Pumpkins together: A SQUASH!!!

Teacher: Of course! The farmer must have planted it in the pumpkin patch by mistake. Well, Olivia, it looks like you have the most unique entry of all. You win!

Lauren: She does? But why?

Teacher: I have never seen a squash-o'-lantern before. That was very clever of you, Olivia!

Olivia: Uh...Thank you!

Eric: Come on. Let's go home and make our pies for the pumpkin pie contest. There's no way they can win that!

Matthew: Well, I wouldn't be so sure.

[*They exit. Olivia and the Ugly Pumpkin put on chefs hats, shake hands, and exit.*]

The End

TEACHER'S GUIDE

The Ugly Pumpkin

Background

Pumpkins are vegetables that are related to squash. Most weigh between 15 and 30 pounds, but some weigh as much as 200 pounds! Pumpkins are a good source or vitamin A and potassium. They can be cooked in many different ways, but the most popular is pumpkin pie. It is fun to make and eat pumpkin seeds, which are filled with protein and iron. Children and adults all over the United States carve pumpkins into jack-o'-lanterns as part of their Halloween celebrations.

Book Links

The All-Around Pumpkin Book by Margery Cuyler (Henry Holt, 1980)

The Biggest Pumpkin Ever by Steven Kroll (Holiday House, 1984)

The Vanishing Pumpkin by Tony Johnston (Putnam, 1983)

Extension Activites

A Pumpkin Poem

Write the following categories on the board: *Look, Sound, Feel, Smell.* Pass a pumpkin among the students. Have them dictate words describing the pumpkin according to each sensory category. Record their contributions under each heading. Cut pumpkin open and repeat activity. Post the list in your writing corner and suggest students refer to the list when writing pumpkin stories and poems.

Visit a Pumpkin Patch

Visit a local pumpkin farm. Before the trip, generate a list of interview questions to pose to the farmers you'll meet there. Prepare to ask farmers, for example, to describe a pumpkin's life from seed to fruit. Have them show students

examples of pumpkin varieties. Which pumpkin types grow the largest? Which pumpkins make the best pumpkin pie? And finally, what weather factors affect pumpkin growth?

Design a Pumpkin

Have students use paper pumpkins to plan jack-o'-lantern designs. Cut out designs to use as stencils to transfer favorite designs to real pumpkins. Help students carve their designs into real pumpkins. When carving your pumpkin, save the cut-out pieces and use as ink-pad stampers for printing jack-o'-lantern features on pumpkin-shaped pieces of paper. After a day or two, steam cook pumpkin shell, scrape the softened pumpkin meat away from the rind and use in your favorite pumpkin recipes.

Feed on Seeds!

Instead of throwing away the seeds from the inside of your pumpkin, roast and eat them! Here's how:

1. Place seeds in a colander and rinse under cold water.

2. Blot seeds dry between paper towels.

3. Spread the seeds in a single layer on a cookie sheet so they are not touching one another.

4. Sprinkle with salt. Bake at 350° for 30 minutes to an hour, or until they are dry and light brown.

A Native American Welcome

by Sandra Widener

Characters:

- Narrator
- Indian 1
- Indian 2
- Squanto
- Samoset
- Edward Winslow
- Elizabeth Hopkins
- Sarah Hopkins
- Massasoit
- Many Indians (nonspeaking roles)
- Pilgrim woman and children (nonspeaking roles)

Props:

- clothing for Pilgrims: simple dresses for the women, pants and shirts for the men, all in bright colors like red, yellow, and purple
- clothing for Indians: straight brown aprons tied around the hips, feather for the hair
- seeds representing wheat and corn kernels
- food (for the Thanksgiving feast)
- table (to hold the feast)

ACT 1

Plymouth, Massachusetts; Spring, 1621.

Narrator: The Pilgrims left England and sailed to North America in 1620 because they wanted to start a new life. That first winter, though, they almost starved. During those months, the Indians who already lived in the area were curious about the newcomers.

[The Pilgrims are on the left side of the stage, shivering and planting wheat kernels by tossing them on the ground. The Indians are on the right side, watching the Pilgrims from behind trees.]

Indian 1: They look cold.

Indian 2: They look hungry, too. Have you watched them plant? Their seeds will never grow.

Indian 1: Should we help them? What if they try to attack us?

Squanto: I know the English. They will not hurt us. Men who attack never bring families. If we don't help them, they will have trouble getting through the rough winter when food is scarce.

Samoset: I agree. I learned their language from other ship captains. Let's talk to them.

[Samoset and the other Indians walk around the trees to greet the Pilgrims, who step back in surprise and fear.]

Edward Winslow: Who—who are you?

Samoset: *[Extending his hand.]* Welcome.

Edward Winslow: *[Shaking Samoset's hand in amazement.]* You speak our language!

Samoset: Yes.

Edward Winslow: *[With a small laugh.]* Well, welcome!

Squanto: We are afraid for you. Conditions are harsh here. I will stay and teach you how to plant corn. I can show you how to catch fish, and which berries to eat.

Elizabeth Hopkins: *[With a frown.]* Why would you do that for us?

Squanto: I do not want to see you starve. I can stay with you because I have no tribe.

Elizabeth Hopkins: *[Smiling at him.]* I think you are the luck we have been seeking in this new land.

ACT 2

An Indian settlement not far from Plymouth Colony, November 1621.

[Squanto walks up to the other Indians.]

Samoset: Squanto! Where have you been?

Squanto: With the settlers. They really needed help! I taught them to plant corn with fish heads, the Indian way. Then I showed them how to get maple syrup from the trees, and which plants to eat.

Indian 1: Their ways are strange.

Squanto: Yes, they are different from us. But they are good people.

Indian 2: I still don't trust them. Other settlers have hurt Indians.

Squanto: Not these people. Besides, I have returned with an invitation. They want us to join them for a feast celebrating their harvest. They have invited the chief, too.

Samoset: A Green Corn festival!

Squanto: I don't know what they call it, but it is a harvest festival like our Green Corn festival.

Indian 1: I'll trust you, Squanto. Let's go!

Indian 2: I'll go, too! And I know some others who would like to come.

ACT 3

The Plymouth settlement, November, 1621. Pilgrim women and children are preparing dinner.

Elizabeth Hopkins: *[Carrying a large pot to the table.]* Quick, children! Bring the cornbread here! Carry that jam to the table!

[Sarah and the other children carry items to the table and then go back to stand near their mothers.]

Edward Winslow: Well, Mistress Hopkins, it will be a fine

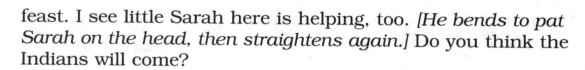

feast. I see little Sarah here is helping, too. *[He bends to pat Sarah on the head, then straightens again.]* Do you think the Indians will come?

Elizabeth Hopkins: I hope so.

Sarah Hopkins: *[Tugging harder at Elizabeth Hopkins's skirt.]* Mother, over there! Look at the Indians coming!

[Elizabeth Hopkins and Edward Winslow turn to see a line of Indians walking toward them.]

Elizabeth Hopkins: *[Gasping.]* There must be 90 of them! What shall we feed them? If we feed them all, we will have no food for winter!

[Squanto and the other Indians walk up to Elizabeth Hopkins and Edward Winslow.]

Squanto: We are pleased to share your feast. I have brought the chief of the tribe.

Edward Winslow: Welcome. Without the help of your tribe and of Squanto, we would not be alive now.

Massasoit: Thank you. *[Looks at the food on the table.]* But I see that you were not prepared for so much help eating your feast! There is not enough to go around.

[Edward Winslow and Elizabeth Hopkins look at each other.]

Elizabeth Hopkins: We will gladly share what we have.

Massasoit: That will not be necessary. *[He nods at the group of Indians.]* They will return with more food.

[The Indians leave.]

Sarah Hopkins: *[Tugging on her mother's skirt again.]* Hey, Mother, when can we eat?

[Everyone laughs.]

Elizabeth Hopkins: She's right. Take a plate, everyone! We'll make do.

[The Indians return, carrying five deer.]

Indian 1: We bring you deer meat.

Edward Winslow: This is a fine gift! You will always be welcome here with us.

Elizabeth Hopkins: We know that without you, there would be no feast—and no harvest.

Sarah Hopkins: *[Her mouth full as she eats an apple.]* No harvest! No food! That's terrible!

[Everyone laughs.]

Elizabeth Hopkins: Let us hope this is the beginning of a long friendship. Happy Thanksgiving, everyone!

The End

TEACHER'S GUIDE

A Native American Welcome

Background

When the *Mayflower* left England in 1620, it carried the hopes of its 102 passengers. Half of them had left to make their fortune in the new world, while the others had broken away from the Church of England and wanted to worship as they pleased. The trip was horrific: one person died and many were sick. The storms were fierce, arguments erupted. Finally, the two groups agreed to begin their life in North America together, and signed the *Mayflower Compact*, which described how they would govern themselves.

Once on the Massachusetts shore, life was no easier. They found cleared land (which they later learned was that of an Indian tribe whose members had died of a European disease) and began constructing their homes on Christmas Day, 1620. The winter was disastrous. By its end, less than half of the Pilgrims were alive, felled by disease and starvation. That spring, when Samoset first uttered his famous "Welcome" in English, he became a loyal and indispensable friend and teacher to the Pilgrims; it is no exaggeration to say that without him, the settlers would not have survived.

Book Links

The First Thanksgiving Feast by Joan Anderson (Clarion Books, 1984)

The First Thanksgiving by Jean Craighead George (Philomel Books, 1993)

The Thanksgiving Book by Lucille Recht Penner (Hastings House, 1986)

Extension Activities

The Peach Stone Game

North American Indians' Green Corn Festival, which is similar to our Thanksgiving celebration, featured not only food, but games and entertainment, as well. The Peach Stone Game was popular during the

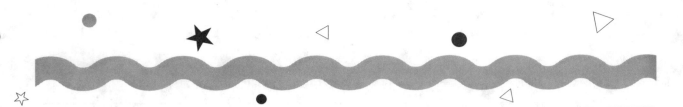

Green Corn Ceremony. It is possible that the Indians and the Pilgrims even played it at the first Thanksgiving. To play, have students paint four clean peach stones with eight different colors, using a separate color on each side of each peach stone. Let each color represent a number. For instance, blue could be three, and red six. Place the stones into a shoe box. Have students take turns shaking the stones in the shoe box. When a student has shaken the box, he or she puts it down and counts the numerical value of the colored peach stones that are laying face up. Have students keep track of their scores to see who the winner is.

Researching Harvest Festivals

As students can tell from the Indians' reference to the Green Corn Festival, Thanksgiving is not the only harvest festival. Have small groups of students research and report on other celebrations that mark the end of the growing season. Books such as Penner's *The Thanksgiving Book*, which has chapters on Thanksgivings elsewhere in the world, will prove helpful. Also, have children report on any family traditions they engage in during the harvest time. Maybe they take an annual outing to pick pumpkins. Or perhaps they celebrate by decorating their homes with autumnal symbols or gather together to tell ghost stories under the Harvest Moon.

The Way to North America

The trip on the *Mayflower* was adventurous—and a huge risk for the passengers. Have students trace the trip, from its launching on September 6, 1620 in Plymouth, England, to the first sighting of land on November 10 at Cape Cod, Massachusetts. Students can (with help, if necessary) not only trace the route on a map, but figure out how long the trip was, and how many miles the ship went on an average day. You might want to discuss how long such a trip would take to complete today.

The Book Brigade

by Paula Thomas

Characters:

- The Book Brigade: The Little Red Hen, The Ugly Duckling, Little Miss Muffet, The Calico Cat, Chicken Little, Cinderella, The Elephant's Child, Mama Bear
- Bailey
- Betsy
- Tina
- Sal

Props:

- one or two pieces of plastic playground equipment
- door (leading to library)
- pieces of oaktag (painted to resemble each character's book or story, and fitted at the top with lengths of yarn or elastic thread so children may hang book shapes around their necks)
- books

ACT 1

A playground located outside a library. One by one members of the Book Brigade walk out of the library and assemble in the playground.

Little Red Hen: This is an Emergency Meeting. Call to order! Now who will help me recite our pledge?

The Book Brigade: *[They join hands and cheer together.]*
The Book Brigade, that's our name.
Getting kids to read is our game.
We live in books and stories and rhymes,
And reach out to kids all the time.

Cinderella: *[To the group.]* Yes, fellow Book Brigadiers, we need to gear up. I've just heard from the head librarian that book withdrawals are down. We all know what that means...*[Group nods and murmurs knowingly.]*

Ugly Duckling: If only those children would just remember to come to the library.

Little Miss Muffet: They just need to check it out, then they'll come more often. Maybe something sat down beside them and frightened them away.

Mama Bear: *[Pointing to the library.]* Check it out, check it out! Come on everybody and check it out!

The Book Brigade: *[Making a single-file line and moving off the playground.]* Check it out, check it out, check it out...

ACT 2

The Book Brigade is outside the library.

The Book Brigade: The Book Brigade that's our name.
Getting kids to read is our game.
Happy or sad, bouncy or blue,
We have just the right book for you!

Mama Bear: *[Pointing to a boy walking on stage.]* Here comes our first customer.

Bailey: *[Dragging his feet as he walks along.]* I'm bored. Bored, bored, bored!

Mama Bear: Do you have a problem young man?

Bailey: Yes, I have a huge problem! I can't watch TV for a week! So what if I play wildly? And what's the big deal if I ask a lot of questions? Why do I have to be in so much trouble! Nobody understands me.

[The Book Brigade huddles, then turns back to Bailey. Cinderella and the Elephant's Child step forward.]

Cinderella: I know exactly where you're coming from. I'm Cinderella. When I lived with my step-mother and step-sisters, no one understood me, either. I used to have to do all the work around the cottage. But, now that I live in the palace with the prince, I just lay around all day reading books and more books.

Elephant's Child: I'm the Elephant's Child. You think that *you* ask a lot of questions and get in trouble? Have you ever been sent to the great, gray, greasy, Limpopo River?

Bailey: You guys make me look dull. Tell me more.

Cinderella: Why don't you read all about us? The rest of our stories are right on the other side of those doors.

Bailey: In the library? That boring place?

Elephant's Child: Don't you want to know the details of Cinderella's rags to riches story? Don't you want to know more about the great, gray, greasy Limpopo River? Don't you? Don't you?

The Book Brigade: *[Whispering and pointing to the library.]*
Check it out, check it out.
That's all you have to do
Check it out, check it out
That'll be the cure for you!

Bailey: I can find out all of that in there? *[Thinks a minute.]* O.K. Let's go. *[Links arms with Cinderella and the Elephant's Child. They walk together into the library.]*

Chicken Little: That last case went well. But, check it out…do you really think that he can stop his sky from falling?

Little Red Hen: He'll be fine! Right now we have more work to do. Now, who will help me greet this child?

[Betsy enters. She is wiping her eyes and crying. She stops to blow her nose.]

Little Red Hen: Why are you crying my dear? Who will help me wipe your tears?

Betsy: *[Sniffling and wiping tears.]* All the kids make fun of me because I lost my two front teeth. It feels like my whole world is caving in. But why should you care? Just leave me alone.

[Book Brigadiers huddle, then the Ugly Duckling and Chicken Little step forward.]

Chicken Little: I know just how you feel. I used to worry about the sky fallin' and crushin' my stuffin'! But I don't worry much about that anymore. *[Glances nervously skyward.]*

Ugly Duckling: And I'm the Ugly Duckling. When I was growing up it was the same with me. Tease, tease, tease.

Betsy: You? Nervous? And, you—a gorgeous swan like you? Ugly? You two are just making those things up to make me feel better.

Ugly Duckling: No, we're not making anything up. I'll prove it! Our stories are right in there. *[Points to the library.]* Read them and make up your own mind.

Betsy: Well, I haven't gone to the library in ages. O.K. Let's give it a try. *[Locks arms with the Chicken Little and Ugly Duckling and they walk into the Library.]*

Mama Bear: *[Pointing off-stage.]* My goodness! I see two more visitors coming our way.

[Tina and Sal saunter on stage talking to each other.]

Tina: Clean up your room! Walk the dog! Feed the cat! Adults are such stick-in-the-muds.

Sal: Really, chores are such a drag!

[Book Brigadiers huddle. The Little Red Hen, Mama Bear, and the Calico Cat step forward.]

Little Red Hen: I'm the Little Red Hen. Who will help me learn your names?

Sal: *[Astonished.]* The Little Red Hen? You mean like the one from the story? *[Gulps.]* Well, I'm Sal and this is Tina.

Mama Bear: Hello Sal and Tina. I'm Mother Bear of Goldilocks fame and this is my friend the Calico Cat.

Calico Cat: Purrfectly charmed, I'm sure. What seems to be your trouble?

Sal: Well, we have to do all these dumb chores around the house.

Tina: It's not fair at all!

Little Red Hen: Too bad Cinderella is already busy. Now there's a girl who knows about dumb chores! All I know is that it's certainly hard to get good help these days. I mean, who *will* help me make the bread?

Calico Cat: Oh just forget your bread, Hen. These kids have their own troubles. *[To children.]* At least you kids don't have to pick up all the stuffing that's laying around my house, what with all the fussing I do with that Gingham Dog.

Tina: What Gingham Dog?

Mama Bear: You mean you don't know about the Gingham

Dog and the Calico Cat? *[Looks knowingly at her Brigade friends.]*

Mama Bear: Come on kids. We know just the way for you to take a refreshing break from all your chores!

[Everyone on stage links arms and walks into the library.]

ACT 3

Book Brigadiers are in the playground, congratulating and giving high fives to one another.

[Bailey, Betsy, Sal, and Tina come out of the library holding the books they have checked out.]

Bailey: I can't stop reading. Cinderella's story gave my life more meaning!

Betsy: *[Laughing.]* These books are awesome. They're the best. Ugly Duckling you're a cut above the rest!

Tina: Calico Cat, your rhyme is just great. Poems and rhymes are really first rate!

Sal: I took a break to meet some old friends. Little Red Hen, I'm glad I read you again!

Bailey, Betsy, Tina & Sal:
Book Brigade you're first rate.
Now it's time to celebrate.
Thanks a million, thanks a ton,
You make reading fun, fun, fun!

Book Brigade: *[Pointing to the library.]*
Check it out,
That's all they had to do. *[Point to the children.]*
Check it out,
Now it's your turn, too!! *[Point to the audience.]*

The End

TEACHER'S GUIDE

The Book Brigade

Background

The earliest American children's literature dates back to the mid 1600's. These grim treatises on proper behavior and the dire outcomes that would befall the naughty child were all that was available until 1744. Then, John Newbery began publishing short tales written specifically to entertain children. This smart businessman found an eager market for his product and the love of children's books has grown ever since. Today children have a cast array of literature to choose from. There are books for leisure and for work, those of prose and those of poetry. To continue fostering the love of books in children everywhere Children's Book Week is celebrated every November. But, remember you can celebrate children's books every day of the year.

Book Links

Alistair in Outer Space by Marilyn Sadler (Prentice-Hall, 1984)

Petunia by Roger Duvoisin (Knopf, 1950)

Simon's Books by Henrik Drescher (Lothrop, Lee & Shepard, 1983)

Extension Activities

Family Favorites

Ask children to interview an adult family member to discover what they read when they were growing up. The family member should name a favorite book or story and tell why the selection is so memorable to them. If possible, have the students find out how the adult first became acquainted with this favorite selection (Did someone read it to them? Did they discover it on their own?). In class, chart the results of your class's investigation. List the responses. How many different types of books and stories were mentioned? Were there any duplicates? What is the most popular book? The most unusual? Are any of the adult's favorites still popular today? Try inviting parents to come in and read their favorites to the class.

Readers as Writers

Read and discuss some of Aesop's fables to the class. Then have the children retell their favorite fables in their own words. Cut blocks of text apart (or if working on a word processor, invite the children to insert page breaks where appropriate) to create sections of text for children to illustrate. Invite children who are willing to share their efforts with the class.

Book Week Bonanza

Set aside one week to celebrate books. Spend time each day of Book Week reading aloud from the children's favorite books. Have a Book Week party. Have each child bring in her or his favorite book, dress as a favorite character from the book, and tell the rest of the class about the book. Serve treats suggested by different stories and poems. Try to have a local author or illustrator come to visit the class during this special celebration. Prepare for the visit by learning all you can about the author, by familiarizing the class with the author's work and by preparing a list of questions to ask during the visit. Follow up with a class thank-you note signed by all the children.

The Hesitant Hibernator

by Cass Hollander

Characters:

- Narrator
- Twin Bear 1
- Twin Bear 2
- Snowshoe Rabbit
- Groundhog 1
- Groundhog 2

Props:

- two cardboard bear masks
- cardboard rabbit mask and cotton tail
- two cardboard groundhog masks
- backdrop of snowy winter woods

ACT 1

The woods in October.

Narrator: Bear cubs are born in January or February. They stay with their mother through the spring, summer, fall, and winter of that first year. Then early in their second summer, they set out on their own. This story is about twin bears on their own for the first time. In June they said good-bye to their mother. They spent the summer fishing, eating berries, and climbing trees. As our story opens, it's October.

Twin Bear 1: Isn't the world amazing? The leaves were green. Then they turned yellow, orange, and red. Now they're falling off the trees—

Twin Bear 2: So are the acorns! *[Scoops up acorns with both paws and gobbles them up.]* Yum!

Twin Bear 1: Stop eating! You're getting fat! You're huge!

Twin Bear 2: I'm a bear! I'm supposed to be huge! *[Tears open a decaying log.]* Wow! Look at all these bugs in this old rotten log! *[Starts scooping up bugs and eating them by the pawful.]* Delicious! Here. Try some. *[Offers the other bear a pawful of bugs.]*

Twin Bear 1: No, thanks. I'm not hungry.

Twin Bear 2: *[Still gobbling bugs.]* You better get hungry! If you don't eat, you're gonna wake up starving halfway through winter. You won't be able to hibernate all winter long.

Twin Bear 1: I've decided not to hibernate this year.

Twin Bear 2: *[Nearly chokes with surprise.]* What? Not hibernate? You *have* to hibernate. You're a bear. It's what bears do.

Twin Bear 1: Haven't you ever wondered what happens in the winter? Aren't you curious?

Twin Bear 2: About winter? No. Let's see if there are any nuts under that tree.

Twin Bear 1: Well, *I'm* curious. I don't want to sleep for four months. That's one third of the whole year. Why should I spend one third of the year asleep?

Twin Bear 2: Because you're a bear. It's what bears do.

Twin Bear 1: Not *this* bear!

ACT 2

The woods in late December.

Narrator: When the last autumn leaf finally fell, and when white flakes fall in soft mounds over all the woodlands, one of our bear friends knew it was time to snuggle deep in a dark, cozy cave and settle down to sleep. But our other bear friend decided to stay awake to see what winter was really like.

Twin Bear 1: This stuff is great! *[Runs around in a circle.]* It's fluffy. *[Rolls on his back in the snow.]* It's fun to roll in. *[Gets up and brushes off fur.]* I wonder what it is. *[Walks down* *stage.]* Look at these things hanging from the tree. *[Breaks an icicle off a fir tree.]* Pretty amazing. *[Puts icicle in mouth.]* Hmmm. Tastes like cold water. I wonder what you call this? *[Looks around. Moves one hind paw around in the snow.]* Winter's nice. But where is everybody?

[Snowshoe Rabbit hops on stage. Sees Bear and starts to hop away fast.]

Twin Bear 1: Wait!

Rabbit: Are you kidding! I'm not going to be your bedtime snack! *[Rabbit hops on one foot then the other to keep warm.]*

Twin Bear 1: What are you talking about? I don't want to eat you! I'm not even hungry!

Rabbit: Then what are you doing up? My mama told me the only reason bears wake up in winter is because they didn't eat enough before they went to sleep. So they get up to find a snack. And I'm *not* gonna be *your* snack!

Twin Bear 1: I didn't get up to find a snack. I didn't get up at all! I'm not hibernating.

Rabbit: Not hibernating? Why not? You're a bear.

Twin Bear 1: I didn't want to miss winter.

Rabbit: What's to miss? It gets cold. The water freezes. There's nothing to eat but bark. I hate it. I'd hibernate if I could. *[Rabbit turns to go.]*

Twin Bear 1: Wait! You're the first living thing I've seen in days. Where is everybody?

Rabbit: Well, some animals are hibernating—like *you* should be. The birds migrated to some place warm. And the rest of us try to stay out of the cold as much as we can. *[Rabbit starts to hop away.]*

Twin Bear 1: Wait! Stay and talk with me.

Rabbit: I'm cold. I hate hopping around in the snow. I'm going home where it's warm.

[Bear looks a little forlorn watching the Rabbit hop away.]

ACT 3

The woods on February 2. Downstage right there's a ground-hog hole with two groundhogs asleep inside. Bear is sitting on a stump near the groundhog hole, looking bored.

Narrator: It's the second day of February. Winter has dragged on for two long, cold months. All that time the ground has been covered with snow.

Twin Bear 1: The worst thing about winter is that nothing happens. There's nothing to do. Nobody's around. *[Holds chin in paw and stares off into space.]*

[Groundhogs start to stir in their hole.]

Groundhog 1: *[Stretching.]* I think I'll take a little walk outside. See what's happening.

Groundhog 2: *[Yawning.]* I'm right behind you. *[Groundhog rolls over and goes back to sleep.]*

[1st Groundhog goes out and sees the Bear sitting on the

stump. Groundhog screams and runs back into the hole. Inside the hole, the other Groundhog wakes with a start when it hears the scream.]

Groundhog 2: What's the matter? Did you see your shadow?

Groundhog 1: No. There's a bear right outside our hole!

Groundhog 2: What's a bear doing up?

Groundhog 1: It must be hungry.

Groundhog 2: Don't go out there again. Let's just go back to sleep. We don't have to get up for another six weeks.

[Bear's twin enters from stage left. Sees Bear on stump.]

Twin Bear 2: *[Approaching Bear on stump.]* Is that you?

Twin Bear 1: *[Jumps up and embraces twin.]* I'm so glad to see you! Is it spring?

Twin Bear 2: I don't think so. I heard some animal scream. It woke me up. I decided to come out and see what was going on. So, how's it going? Are you enjoying winter?

Twin Bear 1: Not really. I liked the snow…at first. But now it's pretty boring. Nothing happens. There's nothing to do. Nobody's around.

Twin Bear 2: Are you ready to hibernate? You've probably got six weeks before winter's over.

Twin Bear 1: I don't think I can take six more weeks of winter.

Twin Bear 2: So, don't. Sleep—the way you're supposed to.

Come on. You can share my cave.

Twin Bear 1: OK. *[Yawns.]* Next year, I think I'll skip winter.

Twin Bear 2: Good idea. You could hibernate winter away. It's what we bears do best!

[Bears exit arm-in-arm, yawning together.]

The End

TEACHER'S GUIDE

The Hesitant Hibernator

Background

Bears usually settle in their dens before the first snowfall and hibernate for the coldest months of the year, December through March. When hibernating, bears do not fall into a very deep sleep the way woodchucks and other hibernating animals do. They are not unconscious and *can* be disturbed. They can wake up to protect themselves. Sometimes they come out of their dens during a warm spell to get something to eat or to just wander about.

The most amazing thing about bear hibernation is the way a bear's metabolism changes. A hibernating bear does not eat, drink or eliminate waste, yet it does not become dehydrated or lose body weight or muscle. This is because the bear's body is able to recycle waste products to maintain muscle tissue and keep the water content of its body in balance.

Book Links

The Mitten: A Ukrainian Folktale by Jan Brett (Putnam, 1990)

The Way of the Grizzly by Dorothy Hinshaw Patent (Clarion Books, 1987)

Wake Me in Spring by James Preller (Scholastic, 1994)

The Winter Bear by Ruth Craft (Aladdin, 1975)

Extension Activities

Where Would They Be?

Read the Russian folktale *The Mitten* by Jan Brett (Putnam, 1990). Research with the children to discover where and how each animal that crawls into the mitten usually spends winter. (One of the animals is a bear, who should have been in his den asleep.) Have the

children make a list of ways they typically spend their winter days and nights. Ask children to tell why they would or would not enjoy hibernating a particular season away.

The Wide World of Bears

Share this poem with your students:

Bear, bear, bear, bear!
How many kinds of bears are there?
Polar bear and grizzly bear,
Big brown bear with lots of hair!
Spectacled bear, black bear too,
Sloth bear, sun bear, quite a few!
Bear, bear, bear, bear!
So many bears to compare.

　　　　　　—by Meish Goldish

After you've read and enjoyed the poem, invite groups of students to research and prepare fact books on one of the types of bears mentioned in the rhyme. When the groups have finished, encourage them to share what they have learned with their classmates. Then add the books to your classroom library for kids to enjoy throughout the year.

Have a Happy Hibernating Party

Invite children to plan a Happy Hibernating party. Encourage them to bring their stuffed bears (and other stuffed creatures) that hibernate to the celebration. Since bears eat a lot before going off to hibernate, food can be an important part of your party. Encourage children to plan a party menu fit for bears, including lots of bear-y good foods such as nuts, berries, and foods made with honey. Encourage the children also to plan appropriate party entertainment such as playing Pin the Tail on the Bear or sculpting bear statues from clay. Collect bear poems, stories, and songs to be shared with the stuffed visitors.

The Mystery of the Missing Munchies

by Sandra Widener

Characters:
- Rachel
- Maria
- Denny
- Melody
- Ray
- Mr. Kramer
- Parents

Props:
- bags with cookies (or pretend cookies)
- other treat boxes and casserole dishes
- two tables
- globe
- chalkboard
- bookshelf with books
- area decorated for a party, including a table, plates, and forks
- index cards printed with mystery clues

ACT 1

Mr. Kramer's classroom, mid-December.

Rachel: Hey, Maria, what are you bringing to the holiday party? I hear there are going to be some tasty munchies for our party.

Maria: *[Looking into a brown paper bag and taking a sniff.]* Rosquillas. They are my family's favorite. Every year at Christmas we make them.

Rachel: *[Looking in the bag, too.]* What are they?

Maria: They're cookies. The best cookies you've ever had!

Denny: *[Holding out a covered casserole.]* Look at this! My mom made bastela. It's from Africa, and it has almonds and custard.

Melody: *[Showing a covered plate of cookies.]* These are sand tarts. My dad says his grandmother ate them when she was a little girl in Sweden.

Rachel: *[Showing her plate.]* Well these are ruggelach, and my mom helped me make them. They have raisins on the inside. We eat them at Chanukah. Are they ever good!

Ray: *[Holding a covered pie plate.]* This is milk flan. It's a kind of pudding. The recipe comes from my grandparents in the Philippines.

Mr. Kramer: *[Walking into the room and looking around.]* Mmmm! Those treats smell delicious! We have to go to lunch now, but we'll all save room for our holiday munchies this afternoon.

[Everyone leaves his or her treats on a table in the room.]

ACT 2

The stage is divided into two parts. One part is Mr. Kramer's classroom, after lunch on the same day, where the children are. In the classroom are a globe, a table, a window, and a bookshelf. The other part of the stage is a room decorated for a party.

Ray: *[Coming over to the table where the treats had been. The table is empty except for a folded piece of paper.]* Oh no! Rachel! Denny! Maria! Melody! Come quick! They're GONE!

Rachel: What's gone?

Denny: Can't you see? The treats for our holiday party! They're gone! They've been stolen!

Melody: *[Looking around.]* No party? No cookies? No nothing? I'm going to cry.

Maria: That won't do any good. *[She leans over and looks at the paper on the table.]* Wait. What's this? *[Maria reads the paper.]* You won't believe this! Whoever took our treats left this note!

Denny: What does it say?

[The children crowd around Maria and the note.]

Maria: It says, "Where the land is green and the water shines blue, you'll find another mystery clue."

Ray: This is making me mad. I just want to eat.

Maria: You can eat as soon as we solve the riddle. Do you have any ideas?

[The children stand around thinking for a few seconds.]

Melody: I know! Could it be a book about the world? *[She runs to the bookshelf and looks.]* No treats here.

Rachel: Where the water shines blue? Hmmmmm.

Maria: Wait a minute! I know! The globe!

[All the children rush to the globe.]

Melody: I sure don't see any treats here.

Ray: Let's look underneath.

[The children lift the globe. Underneath is another note, which Ray holds up and reads.]

Ray: This one says, "Don't be in the dark. You're all so bright. Just walk over and shed some light." What do you think that means?

Maria: Something to do with light. The window? *[She runs over and looks at the glass.]* Nothing there.

Denny: Hey...I bet it's the light switch!

[The children rush to the light switch. Taped underneath is another note. Everyone groans. Denny takes the note down.]

Ray: I still just want to eat.

Rachel: Well, what does this note say?

Denny: This one says, "I can hold more words than you've ever seen. But with one wipe, I come clean."

Ray: I don't want to solve riddles. I want to eat!

Melody: We know, we know. But we can't eat until we find out where the food is, can we?

Ray: OK, then, I'll solve it. "Hold more words." Hmmm...a computer?

Rachel: Somebody's mind?

Maria: No! But, maybe instead of "hold" more words, the poem means "write" more words. What do you write with?

Ray: Pencils, pens...

Denny: It has to be something you can get rid of with one wipe.

Ray and Maria: Chalk!

[The children rush to the chalkboard. Propped on the ledge is another note. Denny takes it.]

Maria: OK, what does this one say?

Rachel: It says, "Keep moving forward! Go to the place where treats are stored!"

Ray: That's easy. Treats belong in my stomach.

Melody: It must be the lunchroom. Come on, everyone!

[The children walk quickly around the classroom and end up at the decorated part of the stage. Mr. Kramer and parents

are there, as well as the pile of treats on another table. The children enter the decorated area.]

Mr. Kramer and the Parents: Surprise!

Maria: Momma! Poppa! What are you doing here! *[Maria and her parents hug.]*

Maria's Mother: Mr. Kramer called and told us he was having a big surprise holiday party for all the children and their parents.

Maria: It sure is a surprise! Thanks, Mr. Kramer.

Mr. Kramer: Everyone was going to bring such wonderful things, I thought it would be fun to share. Look—we have treats from all over the world!

Rachel: Well, you sure surprised us. Good job! And good clues, too.

Ray: OK, OK! Now can we eat?

Mr. Kramer: Of course. Everyone take a plate! Enjoy the munchies! And happy holidays!

The End

TEACHER'S GUIDE

The Mystery of the Missing Munchies

Background

December is a month rich with celebrations. Christmas, Hanukah, and Kwaanza are just a sample of the well-celebrated holidays students' families may be enjoying, and there are many other traditional days to commemorate. Whatever your celebration needs, this play can be customized to reflect your students' particular customs and cultures. You can easily modify portions of the dialogue to reflect your own celebrations and commemorations. You can also take the experience a step farther and have parents or students bake the holiday treats to be used in the play or enjoyed afterwards. Why not use this play as a segue into your own class multicultural fest, with everyone present in the audience joining the cast and the other students for an ethnic celebration?

Book Links

An Ellis Island Christmas by Maxinne Rhea Leighton (Viking, 1992)

Pancho's Piñata by Stephan Czernecki and Timothy Rhodes (Hyperion, 1992)

Seven Candles for Kwaanza by Andrea Davis Pinkney (Dial, 1993)

Hanukah, Oh Hanukah! by Wendy Wax (Bantam, 1993)

Extension Activities

Add a Little Music

When planning a party, plan on including not only ethnic treats but ethnic music, as well. Ask parents and children to bring instruments or recordings to the festivities so they may share holiday songs and music from their individual cultures or backgrounds. Invite

participants to tell why the music is special in their family history or to them personally.

Family Recipe Magic

Have children ask family members to provide copies of favorite family or ethnic recipes to contribute to a Family Recipe Book. Have students copy the recipes onto lined paper. Provide blank pages for children to illustrate with pictures or photos of their families eating the recipes featured. Help children develop captions for their illustrations and photos. Bind pages together into a book and circulate among all the children and their families.

Reporting the Story

Tell children to imagine they are in Mr. Kramer's class and have just had their holiday mystery party. What would they write about it for a school newspaper? How would they describe what happened? Have students illustrate their stories if they wish. (Hint: To guide their reporting efforts, have students study the journalistic structure found in most newspaper features.)

Celebration Graph

Have each student make a list of all the celebrations (including birthdays and family picnics) that they participate in each year. Older students may find it helpful to consult a month-by-month calendar, younger students may find it necessary to complete the exercise at home with the help of family members. Then cover a large bulletin board or hallway with craft paper and create a grid design with a marker. Use the display to graph students' names and all their celebrations (as shown in the illustration). Have students fill in the boxes on the graph with a few words describing one way they commemorate each holiday. What did the children learn about the days and ways they celebrate? Are there any similarities among the children's responses? What accounted for any differences?

Kindness, the Magic Peacekeeper

by Carol Pugliano

Characters:

- Kevin
- Christine
- Grandfather
- Tsao (Sow) Wang
- Tsao Wang's wife
- Child 1
- Child 2
- Child 3
- Dog 1
- Dog 2
- Dog 3
- Emperor

Props:

- rocking chair
- a rock (to represent a dumpling)
- a table and chairs
- plastic tableware
- dog dishes
- paper
- paintbrush

ACT 1

[Grandfather is sitting in a rocking chair. Kevin enters hurriedly, with Christine following.]

Christine: Kevin! Give that dumpling back. It's mine!

Kevin: It is not! Mom gave this to me.

Christine: That's your second one. I saw you sneak it into your pocket after you already ate one.

Kevin: I got an extra one for helping Mom. *[He looks in his hand.]* Oooh, and it looks sooo good!

Christine: Give it to me!

[They begin having a tug-of-war with the dumpling. Grandfather enters.]

Grandfather: Now, now. What's going on here?

Christine: Kevin stole my dumpling.

Kevin: I did not! It's mine!

Christine: It isn't. You are a thief!

Kevin: You are a liar!

Grandfather: Children, you must stop this bickering! After all, tonight is New Year's Eve.

Christine: We know, Grandfather: That's why Mom has been cooking all this great food all week.

Kevin: And she gave *me* this dumpling.

Christine: It's *my* dumpling!

Grandfather: You two should not fight tonight. The New Year must begin with peace, joy, and kindness. In fact, you should be kind to each other all year long. Remember Tsao Wang and his family?

Christine: I remember, Grandfather: They were the happiest family ever.

Kevin: I don't remember that.

Christine: You were probably in the kitchen stealing food when Grandfather told us that story last year!

Kevin: Was not!

Christine: Were too!

Grandfather: Now, now! I would be happy to tell the story again, when you are ready to listen quietly.

Christine: Yes, Grandfather.

Kevin: O.K. We're ready now.

Grandfather: Very well, then. A long, long time ago, there was a man named Tsao Wang.

[Tsao Wang enters and sits.]

He had a very large family and many dogs. They were very happy.

[Wife enters.]

Tsao Wang: Dinner smells wonderful!

Wife: It is all ready. I will get the children.

Tsao Wang: No. You sit down and relax. I will get them.

Wife: Thank you.

Tsao Wang: *[He gets up and calls kids.]* Children! Dinner is ready.

[The children enter and sit.]

Child 1: Yum! That smells great!

Child 2: It sure does!

Child 3: I can't wait to taste it!

Wife: Where are the dogs? They must eat too.

[Child 1 whistles. Dogs come running in. All gather in a semi-circle as if at a dinner table on the floor. Wife begins serving.]

Wife: Here you go, dear. And you, my child, and you, and you. And I can't forget our wonderful pet dogs!

[She serves them as well, but accidentally leaves one out. That dog hangs head.]

Child 1: I have more than my brother/sister. I will share mine with him/her.

Tsao Wang: That is very kind of you. Why aren't the dogs eating?

Wife: Oops. I forgot to give one of them its meal. Here you go.

[Now all the dogs and people begin eating. There is a knock at the door.]

Tsao Wang: I will get it.

Child 3: No, father. I will see who it is. You enjoy your meal.

[He gets up and goes to door. The Emperor enters.]

Child 3: It is the Emperor!

[All stand and bow.]

Tsao Wang: Your majesty. We are honored to have you visit our home.

Emperor: Tsao Wang, I have heard many stories about your family. So many live here in peace. What is your secret?

Tsao Wang: It is really very simple.

Emperor: Could you please write it down so that others can live as happily as you do?

Tsao Wang: Of course.

[He gets a piece of paper and a paintbrush. He writes for a while.]

Tsao Wang: *[Handing the Emperor the paper.]* Here it is.

Emperor: Thank you. *[He looks at paper.]* But you have only written one word over and over: *Kindness.*

Tsao Wang: That is right. *Kindness* is our magic word.

Emperor: Well, I am going to spread this word across the land. Perhaps then everyone in China can live in peace as you do.

[The Emperor leaves. Child 1 gets up and looks out door.]

Child 1: Look at his beautiful carriage!
[All get up to look and exit.]

Grandfather: And to this day, every New Year's Eve, we try to make up with anyone we have fought with and be kind the whole year through.

Christine: But, Grandfather, it is very hard to be kind all the time!

Grandfather: I know, but we must try in little ways with each other every day.

Kevin: Christine, I will share my dumpling with you. I am sorry I called you a liar.

Christine: Thank you, Kevin: I am sorry I called you a thief.

Grandfather: Tsao Wang would be proud of you, and so am I. Happy New Year!

Christine and Kevin: Happy New Year, Grandfather!

The End

TEACHER'S GUIDE

Kindness, the Magic Peacemaker

Background

Chinese New Year is considered the most important of all the Chinese holidays. It usually falls somewhere between the middle of January and the middle of February. Celebrated for more than five thousand years, it marks the end of winter and the beginning of spring. One month before the end of the old year, families begin preparing for the New Year by cleaning their homes from top to bottom. Much food is prepared in advance as stores and markets will be closed during the New Year festivities. The Chinese New Year celebration lasts for five days. These days are filled with feasting, visiting, and parades.

Book Links

Gung Hay Fat Choy: Happy New Year by June Behrens (Children's, 1982)

Chinese New Year by Tricia Brown (Henry Holt, 1987)

Lion Dancer: Ernie Wan's Chinese New Year by Kate Waters and Madeline Slovenz-Low (Scholastic Inc., 1990)

The Magic Boat and Other Chinese Folk Stories by M.A. Jagendorf (Vanguard, 1980)

Extension Activities

The Chinese Zodiac

The Chinese zodiac is a twelve-year cycle. Each year is named for an animal. Each person has an animal sign representing the year of her or his birth. Many Chinese believe that a person's animal sign determines much of his or her personality. To see if this is true for your students and their friends and family members copy the chart below onto a blank bulletin board. Use labeled index cards to match the names of students, friends and family members with the descriptions of the Chinese Zodiac

animals matching their birth year. Have children write essays telling why they believe their Zodiac passages are or are not accurate.

Year of the Boar

1899, 1911, 1923, 1935, 1947, 1959, 1971, 1983, 1995, 2007, etc. People born in this year are very good students. They are honest and brave. They always finish a project or assignment.

Year of the Sheep

1907, 1919, 1931, 1943, 1955, 1967, 1979, 1991, 2003, etc. People born in this year are very good artists. They ask many questions, like nice things, and are very wise.

Year of the Rabbit

1903, 1915, 1927, 1939, 1951, 1963, 1975, 1987, 1999, etc. People born in this year are nice to be around. They like to talk, and many people trust them.

Year of the Monkey

1908, 1920, 1932, 1944, 1956, 1968, 1980, 1992, 2004, etc. Monkey people are very funny. They can always make people laugh. They are also very good at solving problems.

Year of the Snake

1905, 1917, 1929, 1941, 1953, 1965, 1977, 1989, 2001, etc. People born in this year love good books, food, music, and plays. They will have good luck with money.

Year of the Rooster

1909, 1921, 1933, 1945, 1957, 1969, 1981, 1993, 2005, etc. People born in this year are hard workers. They have many talents and think deep thoughts.

Year of the Dragon

1904, 1916, 1928, 1940, 1952, 1964, 1976, 1988, 2000, 2012, etc. Dragon people have good health and lots of energy. They are good friends because they listen carefully to others.

Year of the Rat

1900, 1912, 1924, 1936, 1948, 1960, 1972, 1984, 1996, etc. Rat people are very popular. They like to invent things and are good artists.

Year of the Ox

1901, 1913, 1925, 1937, 1949, 1961, 1973, 1985, 1997, etc. People born in this year are very dependable and calm. They are good listeners and have very strong ideas.

Year of the Horse

1906, 1918, 1930, 1942, 1954, 1966, 1978, 1990, 2002, etc. People born in this year are popular, cheerful, and are quick to compliment others. Horse people can work very hard.

Year of the Tiger

1902, 1914, 1926, 1938, 1950, 1962, 1974, 1986, 1998, etc. Tiger people are brave. Other people respect tiger people for their deep thoughts and courageous actions.

Year of the Dog

1910, 1922, 1934, 1946, 1958, 1970, 1982, 1994, 2006, etc. Dog people are loyal and can always keep a secret. Sometimes dog people worry too much.

Big Words, Strong Words

by Bobbi Katz

Characters:

- Narrator
- Mrs. Alberta King (Martin's Mother)
- M.L. (Martin Luther King, Jr. as a child)
- Mama Williams (grandmother)
- Martin Luther King, Jr. (at age 34)
- A.D. and Christine (King's brother and sister as children)
- Martin Luther King, Sr.
- Crowd

Props:

- dining table
- picket signs reading "FREEDOM NOW" and "VOTING RIGHTS"

ACT 1

Narrator: If you ever go to Auburn Avenue, near the Ebenezer Baptist Church in Atlanta, Georgia, you'll find the boyhood home of Martin Luther King, Jr. Several generations of ministers have raised their families in that house. There's even a bronze plaque with the inscription: MARTIN LUTHER KING, JR. WAS BORN IN THIS HOUSE ON JANUARY 15, 1929. When he was born they called him M.L. At first he was like any other baby, cooing and crying. But soon, anyone could see that little boy was growing into someone special.

The King living room.

Mrs. Alberta King: Come along, children! It's time for us to leave for church. You know Daddy doesn't like us to come in late.

Christine: But Mother, just look at the boys!

Mrs. Alberta King: M.L.! A.D.! Have you been fighting?

M.L.: Mother, A.D. says he's bigger and stronger than I am. But I'm six years old now—I just had to show him I wasn't afraid of him. We were just wrestling a little bit.

Mrs. Alberta King: *[Sighing.]* Now M.L., you should set a good example for your brother. Both of you, wash those messy hands and faces and change your shirts. Mama, will you please help these two little rascals?

Mama Williams: *[Smiling.]* Come along, children, let's go wash up. You don't want to miss a word of Daddy's sermon.

M.L.: *[Changing shirt.]* Mama, what is Daddy preaching about today?

Mama: I'm not sure, M.L. But I bet he'll be urging folks to stand tall—to be the very best they can be! And to meet hate with love.

M.L.: I love *you*, Mama.

Mama: I love you too, M.L. Now let's get going before you and A.D. get into any more mischief.

[Later, same day. The whole family at the dinner table.]

Martin Luther King, Sr.: Hmmm. Alberta, Mama, you sure know how to cook! Fried chicken, collard greens, sweet potato pies. Now this is what I call a feast fit for a king!

M.L.: *[Teasingly.]* That's why the King family is eating it!

Mama: *[Laughing.]* M.L. certainly has a way with words! He takes after his daddy.

M.L.: *[Seriously.]* But Daddy has big words, strong words. When Daddy talks in church, people get all quiet trying to listen. Daddy, can you give me some of those words? Those big words?

Martin Luther King, Sr.: Son, you will have to find your own words. Grow, work hard, study, and you will find them.

M.L.: OK, I will! Mama, Daddy, Mother, A.D., Christine! Listen! I'm going to get me words—big, strong words. Just you wait. I'm going to get them.

ACT 2

Narrator: It's August 28, 1963, in Washington, D.C., and luckily, it's a beautiful day. Over 250,000 Americans from all over the country have come together in the spirit of peace. They have come together, carrying signs demanding equal rights for all Americans. Most of the people are black Americans. But there are many whites among them. Hand in hand, they march to the Lincoln Memorial. The leaders, who have been working hard for civil rights, speak to the sea of people. And then the man who had touched the hearts of fair-minded people throughout the world, comes to the microphone. He puts the speech he has written in his pocket. His words come from his heart.

Martin Luther King, Jr.: *[Folding papers into his pocket.]* Five score years ago a great American signed the Emancipation Proclamation...but a hundred years later...the Negro is still not free...

Crowd: Amen! Amen!

Martin Luther King, Jr.: I say to you my friends...I still have a dream. It is a dream deeply rooted in the American dream! I have a dream that one day this nation...will live out the meaning of its creed: We hold these truths to be self-evident; that all men are created equal. I have a dream!

Crowd: Amen! Amen! Oh yes, Amen!

Martin Luther King, Jr.: I have a dream that my four little children will one day...not be judged by the color of their skin...I have a dream today.

Woman in Crowd: Dream on! Dream on!

Other Voices in the Crowd: *[Cheering.]* Amen! Dream on!

Martin Luther King, Jr.: I have a dream today! Little black girls and little black boys will join hands with little white girls and little white boys and walk together as sisters and brothers. I have a dream today!

Crowd: *[Swaying to the rhythm of the words.]* Yes! Yes! Dream on! Dream on!

Martin Luther King, Jr.: Let freedom ring from the…mountains of New York. Let freedom ring from the…Alleghenies of Pennsylvania. Let freedom ring from Stone Mountain of Georgia, Let freedom ring from Lookout Mountain of Tennessee. Let freedom ring from every hill…of Mississippi. Let freedom ring!

ACT 3

Later that night in a quiet room.

Rev. Martin Luther King, Sr.: Remember when M.L. was little and used to say he was going to get himself some big words. Even then he knew how strong words can be.

Mrs. Alberta King: And he has found the strongest words of all—peace and love.

Rev. Martin Luther King, Sr.: I just hope the people listen with their ears…and their hearts.

The End

TEACHER'S GUIDE

Big Words, Strong Words

Background

Martin Luther King, Jr., always loved words. He learned to read at age four and joined the debating team at high school. In spite of the fact that he was only 5 feet 7 inches tall, he was a good athlete and brought lots of spirit to team sports. At college, King began to study the writings of Henry David Thoreau and Mahatmas Ghandi. Both of these men were willing to go to jail rather than obey unjust laws. King decided nonviolent "passive resistance" might be the answer to gaining equal rights for black Americans. He met his wife, Coretta, while attending graduate school at Boston University. His first job took him to a small church in Montgomery, Alabama. When Rosa Parks, a black woman, decided not to give up her seat on the bus to a white passenger, she was arrested. So King and other leaders organized a successful bus boycott.

Using nonviolent methods in the face of outrageous brutality, King organized civil rights marches throughout the country. Despite strong opposition, President Johnson signed the Voting Act in 1964. King was awarded the Nobel Peace Prize that same year. He was the youngest person ever to receive that honor. On April 4, 1968, he was shot dead by James Earl Ray: The birthday of Martin Luther King, Jr., is now a national holiday. He is the only American who was not a president whose birthday is remembered in this way.

Book Links

Happy Birthday, Dr. King! by Kathryn Jones (Simon & Schuster, 1994)

Martin Luther King, Jr. by Pamela Bradbury and Kathie Billingslea Smith (Simon & Schuster, 1987)

Meet Martin Luther King, Jr. by James T. de Kay (Random House, Inc. 1969, revised 1994)

Martin Luther King, Jr., A Man to Remember by Patricia McKissack (Children's Press, 1984)

Extension Activities

Some Dreams

Talk with students about the difference between King's type of dream and a nighttime dream each student may remember having. After establishing the difference between the two different dream types, encourage the children to express their own personal hopes and dreams for their family, their neighborhood, their country and the world. List the children's dreams under each category on a large piece of chart paper. Transfer each item in the categories on the list to one piece of oaktag. Have students illustrate each of their dreams on the oaktag. Group the illustrated dreams into four separate chapters (as defined by the four categories) and bind the pages into a class book titled "We Have Some Dreams."

Let Freedom Ring

Martin Luther King, Jr., dreamed of freedom for everyone. Discuss with children what freedom means to them. Look the word up in the dictionary. Tell them that the freedom about which King spoke was the freedom for people of all colors and beliefs to make the same choices and receive the same conse- quences (or results) for those choices.

Ask children to tell of some of the choices they make every day involving such routine matters such as:
• eating,
• dressing,
• school work,
• television,
• playing with friends,
• washing and brushing teeth,
• sleeping.

Then have them list the different consequences these choices could generate. (It's quite possible stu- dents—especially young students— aren't aware that they are, in fact, making choices throughout their days, so you might have to point out the consequences for choosing other options they hadn't consid- ered. For example, if all the stu- dents say they brush their teeth, point out that they *choose* to do this with the happy consequence of keeping teeth healthy. But if they choose not to brush their teeth, students might risk receiving the negative consequence of damaging their teeth, upsetting their parents, having cavities filled, etc.) After the idea of choices and consequences has come into a sharper focus, tell children that King wanted all peo- ple to be able to make the same choices of where to live, where to shop and pray, where to sit on public transportation, where to go to school, because before King began to help change laws and people's beliefs, people of color were not offered the same choices with the same consequences as other people.

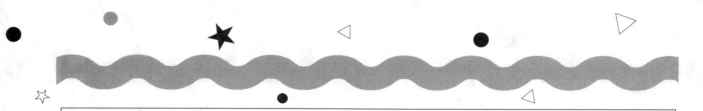

Peacekeepers

Ask children to talk about situations that make them angry and the different ways they have to settle disputes with others. Record any and all possible solutions on a chart. Then, talk with students about how Martin Luther King, Jr., believed that the best way to settle arguments was with peaceful means. Return to your original list. Use a red marker to cross out those solutions students agree are not peaceful or positive. Ask students to regard the remaining items as a list of alternative behaviors they could try when they feel angry enough to strike back with words or deeds. Post the list in the classroom and, when tempers run high, remind the children to check the list before acting. From time to time, add new solutions to the list. Also, discuss with the class how the solutions list is impacting their behaviors.

Dreaming of George and Abe

by Jim Halverson and Carol Pugliano

Characters:

- Andrew
- Lisa
- Marci
- Connie
- George Washington
- Abraham Lincoln

Props:

- two George Washington tri-cornered hats each cut from three construction paper strips stapled together with cotton batting glued on from behind to simulate white wigs
- two Abraham Lincoln hats consisting of top-hat shapes cut from black construction paper and stapled to headbands sized to fit students' heads

ACT 1

The children enter.

Lisa: So what are you guys going to do next Monday?

Marci: Go to school, of course. What a silly question!

Connie: Marci, we don't have school on Monday, remember? It's Presidents' Day.

Marci: Oh yeah. I forgot.

Andrew: I can't wait! It will be great to have an extra day to sleep late and play all day!

Marci: Is that why we have Presidents' Day?

Lisa: No. Presidents' Day is a special holiday to celebrate the birthdays of our two most famous presidents, George Washington and Abraham Lincoln.

Connie: That's right. And I've been thinking of something special we can do for the class. We should put on a Presidents' Day play.

Lisa: That's a great idea! I'll be Abraham Lincoln.

Andrew: And I'll be George Washington.

Marci: What can I be?

Connie: You can be the Narrator.

Lisa: What will you be, Connie?

Connie: The director, of course! Let's go to my house to work on it.

[They exit.]

ACT 2

Connie's house.

[The kids are sitting around. They seem tired. Lisa is wearing an Abraham Lincoln hat and Andrew is wearing a George Washington hat.]

Marci: Connie, we've been working on this play for hours. I'm getting tired.

Andrew: Yeah, Connie: Can't we take a break?

Connie: We want this play to be perfect don't we?

All: *[Tiredly.]* Yeah, yeah...but...

Connie: Then, let's try it again from the beginning. George Washington, you stand there. And Abraham Lincoln, you go there. Marci, stand up front and begin.

Marci: Welcome to our little play
        All about Presidents' Day.
        Our play is short and fun to see
        We'll start with George and the cherry tree.

[Marci steps back and Andrew as George, steps forward.]

Andrew: Once I got a brand new ax.
I loved it so, I couldn't relax.
I chopped at all that I could see
including my father's cherry tree.
When my dad asked me if I knew
who chopped the tree, what could I do?
I said, Dad, I cannot tell a lie—
I felled the tree, I don't know why.

Connie: Excellent! Now you go back to your place.

Andrew: Connie, are you sure that's why we celebrate George Washington's birthday? Just because he told the truth about a cherry tree?

Connie: Of course! I know all about George Washington: We eat cherry pie on his birthday, don't we?

Andrew: I guess so. But didn't he do anything better than just chop a tree down? I mean the whole country celebrates his birthday!

Connie: Never mind. OK, Abraham Lincoln, you're up next.

[Lisa steps forward.]

Lisa: When I was young I was very poor
I had no money, that's for sure.
I lived in a house that was made of logs
We didn't have any cats or dogs.

Connie: Perfect.

Lisa: Connie, this is silly! So, Abraham Lincoln was poor. Is that why we celebrate his birthday? And who cares if he didn't have any cats or dogs?

Marci: Lisa is right. Being poor doesn't seem like much of a reason for Lincoln to be so famous.

Connie: Will you trust me? The play will be great. *[Yawning.]* You know, I'm kinda tired myself. I think I'll just lay down for a minute. Let me borrow your hat. It will help me think better while I rest.

[Connie puts on Lisa's Abraham Lincoln hat and lies down.]

Andrew: *[Lying down.]* That's the best idea I've heard all day!

Lisa: Sounds good to me.

Marci: Me, too!

[They also lie down and all are soon asleep. George Washington and Abraham Lincoln enter. They are more formally dressed than the children.]

Washington: So, Mr. Lincoln, what do you think of the play?

Lincoln: Well, Mr. Washington, it's cute. But I think Connie needs a little bit more information.

Washington: I agree. Let's talk to her.

[Washington and Lincoln approach Connie who is asleep. Lincoln gently nudges her.]

Connie: Wha...? Huh...?

[Connie screams and stands up abruptly. She and Abe are face to face. They do some mirroring of each other. She touches her hat and Abe touches his. She lifts her hat off,

Abe lifts off his. She puts her hat back on, so does Abe.]

Lincoln: Hello, Connie.

Connie: AHHH!!! Who are you?

Lincoln: I'm Abraham Lincoln. I'd like you to meet George Washington.

Washington: *[Shaking Connie's hand.]* How do you do?

Connie: *[Disbelievingly.]* Hello. What are you doing here?

Washington: We heard about your play. We think you should know a little bit more about us before you continue.

Connie: You do?

Lincoln: Yes. It's true that George Washington here was a very honest man. But he did many other wonderful things that you celebrate on Presidents' Day.

Connie: Like what?

Lincoln: Well, Mr. Washington helped to make our country free. He also became the very first President of the United States. He's known as the Father of Our Country.

Washington: Well, thank you, Mr. Lincoln, my good man.

Lincoln: You're welcome. I've always been a big fan of yours, you know.

Washington: Well, thank you. But, Mr. Lincoln, you were a pretty great man yourself.

Connie: He was? What did he do?

Washington: Mr. Lincoln believed that all people should be treated equally, no matter what color their skin was. He helped to free the slaves.

Connie: Wow. That *is* great!

Lincoln: Well, we don't mean to brag. We just want you to put on a play that really helps other children learn facts about why they're celebrating our day.

Washington: Yes. The stories you tell in your play are fun but they're not all that children should know.

Connie: Well, thanks for your help, Mr. Washington and Mr. Lincoln.

Lincoln: You're welcome. Now why don't you lay back down and finish your nap?

[He removes his hat and helps Connie lay down.]

Washington: Yes, great playwrights need their rest. Good-bye!

[They exit. Abraham leaves his hat behind.]

Connie: *[Laying down.]* Good-bye.

[The other children stir and wake up.]

Marci: What a great nap!

Andrew: Yeah. I feel much better.

Lisa: Connie, wake up! Let's get back to work.

Connie: OK, Mr. Washington: Huh? Oh, you guys, you

missed it! George Washington and Abraham Lincoln were just here!

Andrew: Oh, Yeah? Right! Like we believe you!

Lisa: You must have been dreaming!

Connie: But it was so *real*. They told me all about themselves. Now that I know what great men they really were, I'm going to rewrite the play to tell about their great deeds!

Marci: Wow. What was it like to talk with them?

Connie: It was great. Too bad it was just a dream... *[She picks up Abe's hat that she just notices.]*... or was it?...

The End

TEACHER'S GUIDE

Dreaming of George and Abe

Background

George Washington, born on February 22, 1732, in Virginia, was Commander-in-Chief during the Revolutionary War and chairman of the committee that wrote the Constitution. In 1789, George Washington became our nation's first president. The tradition of celebrating George Washington's birthday began even before he became president. While Washington and his army were at Valley Forge, Pennsylvania in 1778, a small celebration took place at his headquarters in the snow. Although his soldiers were hungry and cold, an army band marched and played for him.

The biggest Washington's birthday celebration took place in 1932, 200 years after Washington's birthday. A committee was formed by Congress to plan a period of festivities which was to last from February 22 to Thanksgiving. At that time many streets and squares were renamed for him.

In 1809, Abraham Lincoln was born in a log cabin in what is now Hodgenville, Kentucky. He grew up a farm boy. Lincoln had less than a year of formal schooling, but he was dedicated to educating himself. In 1861, Abraham Lincoln became the 16th President of the United States. He served until he was assassinated in 1865. His story has inspired millions of people of all ages. The first formal observance of Lincoln's birthday was held in the Capitol building in Washington, D.C., on February 12, 1866. In 1892, Illinois became the first state to legalize the holiday.

The centennial of Lincoln's birthday in 1909 seemed to launch the establishment of the day becoming a national holiday. In New York City, there was a special dinner in honor of Lincoln. One of the dinner guests was a former slave named Booker T. Washington. Mr. Washington told the group that his mother prayed that Lincoln would free the slaves. Celebrating Lincoln's birthday was celebrating the answer to his mother's prayer.

Book Links

George Washington by Edgar and Ingri D'Aulaire (Doubleday, 1936)

A Picture Book of George Washington by David A. Adler (Holiday House, 1989)

Washington's Birthday by Clyde Robert Bulla (Harper, 1967)

Abraham Lincoln by Edgar and Ingri D'Aulaire (Doubleday, 1987)

Lincoln: A Photobiography by Russell Freedman (Ticknor, 1987)

A Picture Book of Abraham Lincoln by David A. Adler (Holiday House, 1989)

Extension Activities

Play It Again

Working together as a class, write the play that Connie might write now that she knows more about George Washington and Abraham Lincoln: Record the lines of the play on a large piece of chart paper or just allow children to improvise lines. Use this play-writing opportunity to help children become acquainted with the other parts of the play such as the list of characters, settings, props, and stage directions.

Elect to Vote

Review with students an elected official's roles and responsibilities. At local election time, acquaint students with the candidates and their platforms. Visit a real voting booth to see how it operates. Back in class, section off a corner of the room to serve as a booth where students may cast votes for their favorite candidates. Invite voters to write down their choices on ballots and drop the ballots into a slot cut in the lid of a cardboard box. Form a committee to count the ballots and announce the majority's choice. Students may also elect to use this democratic voting process to make real-life classroom decisions, such as what book to read or what theme unit to study.

Memorable Memorials

• Bring in pictures of different landmarks dedicated to past presidents. The Lincoln Memorial, Washington Monument, Kennedy Space Center, and Mount Rushmore are some examples. Help students find the location of each landmark on a map. Discuss why monuments and memorials are built. Ask kids to think of a person for whom they might want to build a monument. Have them use blocks and other building manipulatives to create models of their memorials.

• Provide students with a collection of various coins and bills. Before

displaying the money, ask students if they know which President (or other famous face) is on each bill and coin. After students examine and identify the money, make a chart that shows who is on the bills and coins and what they are worth. Then offer children the chance to design money featuring someone they admire.

• After someone has been elected to a political office, it is his or her job to represent all people. After noting current affairs addressed in newspapers and magazines, brainstorm a list of issues that interest students. Then encourage them to send their thoughts on these issues to the President of the United States. Help students write their own individual letters or take a vote on one particular issue and compose a collaborative message. Send your letters to:

The President
The White House
1600 Pennsylvania Avenue
Washington, DC 20500

If students write individual letters, they will receive a picture of the President and a postcard message. If the class writes a letter, the teacher and class will receive a packet which includes a poster, a letter to the students, and a letter to the teacher.

The Magic Ring

by Deborah Kovacs

Characters:
- Narrator
- Abu: a boy
- Amokye: his mother
- Dog
- Cat
- Kwasi: a chief (first appears as a pigeon)
- Ananzi: the trickster spider
- Yaa: Ananzi's niece
- Members of the Kwasi's tribe
- Mouse
- Mouseling
- Fish

Props:
- a cage
- a crown
- a cape
- a spear
- a ring

ACT 1

The road home from the market.

Narrator: Abu lives with his mother on a small plot of land at the edge of a village in Africa. Poor and honest, they work hard to grow yams, sell them at the market, and live on what little they earn. Abu is a good son, but he sometimes acts without thinking. This story tells about a time he sold his yams for one gold coin and then makes a foolish trade when, on the way home, he meets a girl carrying a pigeon in a cage. He does not know that the girl is really Yaa, the niece of Ananzi, the trickster spider.

Yaa: *[Disguised as a girl/whispering to the audience.]* I want that gold coin. How can I get it?

Abu: That's a nice pigeon!

Yaa: Would you like to buy it?

Abu: How much?

Yaa: One gold coin.

Abu: I've always wanted a pigeon. *[He thinks, then decides.]* Here. *[He gives the coin to Yaa.]*

Narrator: The girl hands the pigeon cage to Abu, and disappears in a puff of smoke.

Abu: *[Surprised.]* Where did she go?

Pigeon: Help!

Abu: *[Surprised again.]* Who said that?

Pigeon: I'm not a pigeon at all! I am Kwasi!

Abu: You mean, the chief from the next village who disappeared!

Pigeon: Yes! Ananzi turned me into a pigeon! Please set me free!

Abu: But...all right. *[He opens the cage.]*

Pigeon: *[Flying away.]* Thank you! I won't forget this!

ACT 2

Ananzi's cave.

Narrator: Upon returning home, Abu tells his mother, Amokye, that he spent his money for a pigeon that flew away. Amokye cries at the bad news. She's afraid now they will have nothing. Abu is ashamed and sorry. Meanwhile, in Anazi's cave, Ananzi is very angry at Yaa for selling Kwasi.

Ananzi: *[Angrily.]* How could you sell Kwasi! Now we will never get his magic ring!

Yaa: *[Hanging her head.]* I'm sorry, Uncle!

Ananzi: We must try to get that ring some other way!

ACT 3

Abu and Amokye's cottage.

Narrator: Kwasi and his tribe come to thank Abu for giving him his freedom.

Kwasi: *[Holding out ring.]* You have given me my freedom. In return, I give you this magic ring, which will grant all your wishes.

Abu: *[Amazed.]* Thank you!

Narrator: Abu uses the ring's power to build a new home for himself and his mother, and to give them fine clothes to wear. Ananzi soon finds out what had become of the magic ring. One night, when Abu is sleeping…

Ananzi: *[Creeping into Abu's room and snatching the ring.]* Ha, ha, ha! The ring is mine!

Narrator: The next morning, Abu finds himself once more living in a hut, dressed in rags.

Abu: What happened? Where is the ring?

Narrator: Abu's pet dog and cat suspect the truth.

Cat: Let's go get that ring back.

Dog: Ananzi can't do this!

ACT 4

Ananzi's cave. Cat and Dog are peering in.

Dog: I'm scared to go in there. What if he turns us into pigeons?

Cat: Leave this to me.

Narrator: The cat sees a mouse and a mouseling about to enter the cave. Quick as a flash, she puts her paw down on the mouseling's tail.

Mouse: Get your filthy paw off my little mouseling!

Cat: I will, if you will go inside the cave and bring out the magic ring.

Mouseling: Hurry, mother!

Narrator: The mouse has no choice. She scurries into the cave, snatches the ring and brings it back.

Mouse: Here is the ring.

Cat: Here is your mouseling.

ACT 5

A river bed running between Abu's hut and Ananzi's cave.

Narrator: The cat and the dog hurry back to Abu's hut. Meanwhile, Ananzi wakes up and finds the ring missing.

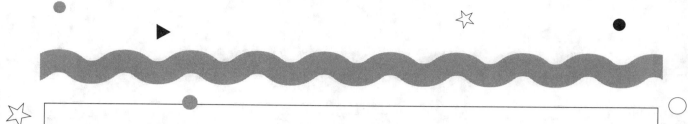

With his spider sense, he follows the trail of the cat and the dog.

Ananzi: They will not cross the river alive!

Narrator: He makes the river rise high, in a great flood.

Cat: Can we make it?

Dog: Sure! Give me the ring! I'll hold it in my mouth.

Narrator: The dog and the cat swim for all they are worth. Halfway across, the dog is exhausted. He opens his mouth wide to catch his breath...and the ring falls out.

Dog: Oh, no!

Narrator: The ring drops to the river bed. A fish swallows it.

Fish: *[Surprised.]* What was that?

Narrator: The dog crawls up on the shore, exhausted.

Cat: We can't go back without that ring! I'm going to get it!

Narrator: The cat dives down to the river floor. It finds the fish that swallowed the ring. It gives the fish a big hug...

Fish: Urrrrppp!

Narrator: And out pops the ring!

Dog: You did it!

ACT 6

Scene 1

Abu's hut.

Narrator: They rush back with the ring to Abu's hut.

Abu: The ring! We are saved! How can I thank you?

Cat and Dog: *[Panting.]* Use the ring to catch Ananzi!
Abu: Great idea!

Scene 2

Ananzi trapped in "pigeon cage."

Ananzi: I'll get you for this, Abu!

Narrator: For now, at least, Ananzi's tricks are over.

The End

TEACHER'S GUIDE

The Magic Ring

Background

The villain in this story, Anansi the spider, is a very familiar figure in folktales of the Ashanti and Akan peoples of Ghana in Central Africa. Also called Kwaku (Uncle) Anansi, stories of his exploits sometimes depict him as a hero, and sometimes as a buffoon. He is usually shown in conflict with other creatures, endlessly trying to outwit them. Though he is sometimes described as a wise man, he is more usually sneaky or greedy and unprincipled. Some tales of Anansi offer explanations for natural phenomena (such as the phases of the moon) or the origins of Ashanti traditions and customs.

Trickster figures, perhaps descended from Anansi, figure prominently in many African-American folktales, where they are known by many names, including B'rer Rabbit and Aunt Nancy. These tales came to America when Africans were forced to come to this country and were sold into slavery. Commemorate Black History Month, which falls in February, by sharing one of these wonderful stories—"The Magic Ring"—in play form.

Book Links

The Days When the Animals Talked: Black American Folktales and How They Came to Be by William J. Faulkner (Follett, 1977)

A Treasury of African Folklore by Harold Courlander (Crown, 1975)

A Treasury of American Folklore, edited by B.A. Botkin (Crown, 1944)

The People Could Fly: American Black Folktales by Virginia Hamilton (Harcourt, 1985)

Extension Activities

Tricksters Today

Trickster tales have been told for thousands of years and are still

told today. In the same way that some Anansi stories paint him as a hero and others as a villain, some modern-day tricksters are heroes (such as Bugs Bunny) and others are villains (such as Wyle E. Coyote). Discuss the definition of a trickster with students. Ask: Are there such things as good and bad tricks? What about good and bad tricksters? Have students make a list of all the tricksters they can think of, including those featured on television and those found in literature. Have students decide if the tricksters mean well or not, and have them offer possible explanations for their motives.

Tellers of Tales

Until about 100 years ago, most African-American folktales were passed down orally. In this century, a number of talented writers collected these stories and wrote them down. Your students may want to read the writing of such folktale collectors and retellers as Zora Neale Hurston, Langston Hughes, Ashley Bryan, and Virginia Hamilton. After hearing some of these stories read aloud, students might want to return to the oral tradition by practicing learning and retelling these stories for an audience.

Just-for-Fun Spider Treats

For each treat, you will need:
• an individual graham-cracker pie crust (available commercially)

• chocolate pudding
• two candy-coated chocolate candies
• 6 thin, black licorice shoestrings, cut to 3 1/2 inches each

Spoon pudding into pie crust. Insert licorice laces into each side of the pudding pie (three on each side) so that each lace drapes over the side of the crust. Press eyes into place.

Thank You, Mr. Bell!

by Carol Pugliano

Characters:

- Caller 1
- Caller 2
- Messenger
- Party Guest
- Party Giver
- Alexander Graham Bell
- Tom Watson
- Mom

Props:

- two toy telephones
- old-fashioned clothing for Bell and Watson

ACT 1

[Caller 1 and Caller 2 are seated in front of classroom/stage pretending to be on the phone.]

Caller 1: Hello?

Caller 2: Hi, *(insert child's name)*. This is *(child's name)*. I have been trying to call you all day! Your line has been busy.

Caller 1: I was on the phone. I'm having a birthday party on Saturday and I was inviting all my friends. Wanna come?

Caller 2: Sure. Boy, you must have a lot of friends since you were on the phone so long! Why didn't you just send out party invitations in the mail?

Caller 1: The party is in a few days. The mail would take too long. The telephone is faster.

Caller 2: I guess you are right. You should thank Mr. Bell!

Caller 1: Who?

Caller 2: Alexander Graham Bell. He invented the telephone.

Caller 1: Guess I should thank him for that. I can't imagine living without a phone.

Caller 2: Well, people used to do it. But it was a lot of work trying to send messages.

[The messenger approaches the party guest at one end of the classroom/stage.]

Messenger: (*Insert party giver's name*) wants you to come to his/her birthday party on Saturday.

Party Guest: Oh, great. What time?

Messenger: I don't know. I'll find out.

[The messenger travels completely to the other end of the classroom/stage to the party giver.]

Messenger: (*He/She*) wants to know what time the party is.

Party Giver: It will be at 2 o'clock.

[The Messenger trudges all the way to the party guest as though out of breath.]

Messenger: The party is at 2.

Party Guest: Is that AM or PM? And should I bake some cookies for the party?

Messenger: I'll find out.

[The messenger walks more tiredly back to the party giver.]

Messenger: Would you like him/her to bake some cookies for your party?

Party Giver: That would be very nice.

[The Messenger laboriously walks back towards the Party Guest, but collapses mid-way.]

Caller 1: Things were sure different back then! But how did Mr. Bell invent the telephone?

Caller 2: Alexander Graham Bell wanted to make things that made life easier for people. He thought it would be great if people could talk to each other over a wire. He and his partner, Tom Watson, worked hard every night trying to figure it out. But things were not going so well. Until one night…

Tom: We have been working for months and nothing is happening!

Alexander: I know Tom, but we must keep trying. I will go into the next room. I will say a few words and you tell me if you can hear me.

Tom: OK. I'll be waiting.

[Tom pretends to hold a receiver to his ear as he waits. Alexander goes to the other side of the room/stage.]

Alexander: *[Pretending to speak into a phone.]* Mr. Watson. Come here. I want you.

[Tom screams and comes running into the room where Alexander is.]

Tom: I heard you! I heard you!

Alexander: What did I say?

Tom: You said "Mr. Watson. Come here. I want you."

Alexander: WE DID IT!!!!

[They give each other high fives and run off excitedly.]

Caller 1: So that's how it happened?

Caller 2: Yes. People were very excited about the telephone. It changed their lives!

[Mom enters.]

Mom: *[Speaking to Caller 1.]* Are you still on that phone? You have been talking all day! Hang up and help me set the table for dinner.

Caller 1: Yes, Mom. *[Mom exists.]* Well, I gotta go. Thanks for the lesson.

Caller 2: Don't thank me. Thank Mr. Bell. Bye!

Caller 1: Bye! *[Replaces receiver and pats phone gently.]* And thanks to you, Mr. Bell.

The End

TEACHER'S GUIDE

Thank You, Mr. Bell!

Background

The man we know as Alexander Graham Bell was born in Edinburgh, Scotland, on March 3, 1847. He was born Alexander Bell and took on the middle name, Graham, when he was 11 years old. He wanted to distinguish himself from his father and grandfather who had the same name. Along with sharing their names, Alexander Graham Bell also shared his relatives' interest in speech and language. His grandfather was an expert on speech impediments. His father was a speech teacher who became well-known for "Visible Speech," a special kind of alphabet used by deaf people in learning how to speak.

Young Alexander was always trying to figure out how things worked. He became a teacher of the deaf in Boston, Massachusetts, but would tinker with inventions in the evening. While he was proud of his invention of the telephone, he always said he would have preferred to be known as a teacher of the deaf. He was the person responsible for arranging for Annie Sullivan to become Helen Keller's teacher.

There were about 10 million phones in service when Alexander Graham Bell died on August 2, 1922. Today there are more than 425 million telephones being used all over the world!

Book Links

Alexander Graham Bell by Richard Tames (Franklin Watts, 1990)

Hello, Alexander Graham Bell Speaking by Cynthia Copeland Lewis (Dillon Press, Inc., 1991)

Thomas Alva Edison: Young Inventor by Louis Sabin (Troll, 1983)

What Has Wild Tom Done Now? A Story of Thomas Alva Edison by Robert Quackenbush (Prentice, 1981)

Extension Activities

Telephone Tunes

Alexander Graham Bell was a very accomplished musician. He almost became a concert pianist! If there were touch-tone phones back in his day, he would have enjoyed using the buttons to emit musical tones. These tones can actually play songs for students to enjoy! After getting permission to use the phone, students should call a friend willing to stay on the line while the songs are being played. (Otherwise, they may accidentally place a phone call.) Each child can take turns playing a song for the other or both can play a duet! Here are two push-button telephone tunes:

Mary Had a Little Lamb

6 2 1 2 6 6   6
Mar-y had a lit-tle lamb

2 2 2   6 6   6
Lit-tle lamb, lit-tle lamb

6 2 1 2 6 6   6
Mar-y had a lit-tle lamb

6   2   2   6   2   1
Its fleece was white as snow.

Happy Birthday

1   1   2   1   # 6
Hap-py birth-day to you

1   1   2   1   # 3
Hap-py birth-day to you

1   1   #   #   8 4 1
Hap-py birth-day dear (na-me)

6   4 2 1
Hap-py birth-day to you

Make Your Own Telephone

You will need:
2 paper cups, 2 paper clips, scissors, string.

What to do:
1. Poke a hole in the bottoms of the cups.
2. Cut a piece of string about 25 feet long.
3. Pull one end of the string through the bottom of one cup.
4. Fasten a paper clip to the string inside the cup. Tie a knot in the end of the string. This will keep the string in place.
5. Repeat steps 3 and 4 with the other paper cup and the other end of the string.
6. Each partner holds a cup, and they walk away from each other so the string is taut.
7. One person holds the cup to his or her ear while the other person talks into the cup at the opposite end of the string.

You can substitute plastic cups, tin cans, or oatmeal boxes for the paper cups. Also try substituting wire, ribbon, or rope for the string. See if these substitutions make any difference in the sound transmission.

Student partners can re-enact the excitement felt by Bell and Tom Watson when they first communicated through a wire by making their own phone.

Play a Game of "Operator"

A game of Operator, sometimes known as Telephone, is a great way to enhance students' listening skills. It is also a good test of how well a child can retain information. Have students sit in a line or a circle. Make sure they sit far enough apart so that they can't overhear what other students are saying. Whisper a sentence into one student's ear. Then have that child pass the message on to the child sitting next to him or her. That child passes the message on, and so on. If someone doesn't understand the message, they say "Operator" and the message is repeated. The last child to receive the message says it out loud. See how jumbled a message can get when it goes through many sources. Alexander Graham Bell's invention helps us avoid such confusion!

In Like a Lion, Out Like a Lamb

by Mary Beth Spann

Characters:

- Narrator (adult or older student)
- The Lion-like North Wind/The Lamb-like Spring Breeze (played collectively by any number of students)
- Dark gray winter cloud/sun
- Snowflakes/Flowers (played by any number of students)
- Woodland Animals: squirrels, chipmunks, rabbits, (played by any number of students)

Props (optional):

- paper leaves (cut from red, orange, and yellow construction paper)
- paper icicles (cut from blue construction paper)
- paper leaf buds (cut from green construction paper)
- length of brown craft paper (running across entire length of stage), cut lengthwise to represent uneven ground line (approximately 3 feet high) for characters to "burrow" behind. This paper ground line may be taped upright against student chairs placed a few feet apart.

129

Props/Costumes (continued):

- Help children design paper-plate stick puppets to serve as simple masks representing the characters in the play. As they perform the play, they can hold the puppet masks as they go through the movements. (Tip: Since nature is depicted as characters in this play, this is a good opportunity to introduce students to the concept of personification in literature.) Consider adding ribbons or crepe-paper streamers to the masks representing the wind and the water.

- A supply of paper-plate spring flower masks can be hidden behind the craft-paper ground line. Students playing the snowflakes can "melt" and then exchange their snowflake masks for spring flower masks.

- To prepare the student trees, tape autumn leaves to their "branches." Then place a supply of paper icicles and paper leaf buds nearby for the wind to tape to the branches at the appropriate times.

Pantomime Production Notes:

- The action words in italics in the following pantomime play suggest movements the students may act out. Before asking the children to pantomime any movements suggested by the story, have them listen as you read through the entire story line. Then print the underlined words on a piece of chart paper. As you familiarize students with the list, encourage them to suggest a variety of ways they might use movements to depict each action. Be prepared to offer some ideas of your own—especially for those movements that children may find difficult to envision. Jot any movement ideas in parenthesis next to the words on the list, for example:

darkened: hunch shoulders, lift elbows, and cover face with hands

bubbled and foamed: bend the knees up and down standing in place

icy gusts: make large circles across the front of the body with the arms

felt quite powerful: puff up chest, throw shoulders back

give up hope: throw hands up in despair

melted over to nibble: slither body down and up again

scurried over to hear: run with tiny, hurried steps

swirled up to nudge away: flutter wrist upwards

ACT 1

The Winter Woodland.

Narrator: It was the beginning of March, the dead cold of winter. Each day, a cheerless cloud *darkened* the sky as the powerful North Wind *roared* across the woodland like a huge lion with razor-sharp icicle teeth. Ever since the first snowflakes of winter first *drifted* down in November past, North Wind could not be stopped.

[Students representing snowflakes can begin swirling around and then moving more furiously on stage as the wind whips them around. Also, if you have opted to use paper-plate snowflakes, a few of these may be placed in front of the ground line to simulate snow piling up.]

All winter long, the wind *ripped* a frozen path through the woods, *slamming* this way and that, leaving crusty layers of ice and snow in its wake. Trees that once *stood tall* with branches full of colorful autumn leaves, now *hung low* with sharp, glassy icicles. *[Students playing the wind take away taped-on autumn leaves and replace them with icicles.]* Streams and brooks that once *bubbled and foamed* were *frozen* into solid ribbons of ice; woodland animals that once *scampered* in the warm autumn sun, now *huddled together* in the stone-cold ground to escape the wind's force; flowers that once *swayed* in the autumn air now *lay quiet and bent* beneath the silent weight of the frosty snow. Even the children, who, in November, *had dangled tongues and mittens* in the air trying to catch the first snowflakes of winter, now lowered their heads and squinted against the *icy gusts* that *bit* into their faces.

By mid-March, North Wind thought it time to *swirl about* and survey its work. It *licked its icy lips* and *smiled a frosty smile* as it *glared* at the frozen land. North Wind knew it had helped to freeze the woods over, and it *felt quite powerful*, indeed! All the woodland plants and animals—and even the children who played there—were about ready to *give up hope* that the spring thaw would ever arrive.

And then, at the end of March, just when the whole world—including all the hope and promise—seemed to be forever frozen still and lifeless, a tiny springtime surprise *popped up!* The trees *stretched over to see* it. The frozen waters *melted over to nibble* at it. The woodland animals *scurried over to hear it*. The children *bent near* to *smell it*. And together everyone was *feeling the same sense of wonder* for a velvety crocus flower—the very first flower of springtime—*had managed to push* its fresh, flowery face up through the sparkly snow.

Everyone began *shouting hoorah!*—that is until the North Wind *spotted* the tiny bud, *drew in its breath*, *bent down* dangerously close to the fledgling flower and tried *blowing* a blustery wind against the delicate petals. But, much to North Wind's *surprise*, all that came out was a whisper-soft spring breeze, warm and gentle as a baby lamb's breath. The breeze *touched* the bud's petals and then *swirled up to nudge away* the dark winter clouds that *hung* above. Suddenly the woods were *bathed* in sunlight. The new bud *turned* its petal face toward the light. Meanwhile, more and more flower buds began *popping up* everywhere! Snow and ice *melted* into liquid streams and brooks. Animals *hopped* out of their hiding places to *stretch and scamper* at last. Icicles on the trees *melted*, leaving tiny leaf buds on the tree branches. *[Students playing the wind can now replaced the taped-on icicles with taped on leaf buds.]* Children *peeled off* their winter mittens, boots, and hats so they could *run* and *play* spring games. By the time March turned into April, the whole woodland was *dancing around* to celebrate the new spring season—especially the lamb-like spring breeze who had once blown fierce as a lion in winter.

The End

TEACHER'S GUIDE

In Like a Lion, Out Like a Lamb

Background

The story of "In Like a Lion, Out Like a Lamb" offers students a fanciful, metaphorical look at how weather and wind change as Earth says good-bye to winter and hello to spring. In reality, the changing seasons are due primarily to the combined factors of the Earth's tilted position on its axis and its orbit around the sun. This accounts for the differences in the amounts of heat received from the sun at different times of the year. The more direct the rays from the sun, the warmer the weather over a period of time. Long days and direct rays make for a summer season; short days and slanted rays make for a winter season. Spring and autumn are transitional periods between the extremes. Earth's lopsided trip around the sun is not only responsible for changes in the seasons, but for other phenomena like wind, rain, and life cycles evident in plant and animal life.

Book Links

Catch the Wind by Gail Gibbons (Little Brown, 1989)

It's Raining Cats and Dogs: All Kinds of Weather and Why We Have It by Franklyn M. Branley (Houghton Mifflin, 1987)

When the Wind Blew by Margaret Wise Brown (Random House, 1979)

Extension Activities

Lion-into-Lamb Books

Provide each student with a lion-shaped piece of construction paper and a lamb-shaped piece of construction paper. Also, provide each student with one piece of manila paper that has been cut in half lengthwise. Help students tape the manila paper end to end and then tape one end to the lion's head. Fold the manila paper accordion-style so that the folds are

concealed behind the lion's head. Tape the lamb's head to the other end of the folded manila paper, thus creating an accordion fold-out book. Students may use the book to draw and label scenes from the pantomime play. Or they may use one side to record signs of winter and the other side to record signs of spring.

Signs of Seasonal Changes

Help children sharpen their observational skills by taking them on indoor and outdoor walking trips designed to help them notice any seasonal changes around them. Focus students' attention on changes evident in three or four observable areas in your school or surrounding neighborhood. For example, students may be asked to observe changes in foliage, shop windows, people's outdoor dress, people's outdoor activities, seasonal or holiday decorations, etc. Record students' observations on chart paper. Post the papers on the walls and decorate the borders with snapshots showing students engaged in seasonal happenings. Refer to the charts to remind students of the way things were before looking for new changes to the viewscape.

Bulb Gardens

Visit your local nursery and ask the personnel to help you raise a "forced bulb garden" in your class-room. Many students are not familiar with planting bulbs and will delight in an up-close look at bulbs and how they are raised. Also, think ahead and consider planting bulbs outdoors with students in the fall so they can really look forward to discovering the first sprouts of spring.

An Earth Day Carol

by Paula Thomas

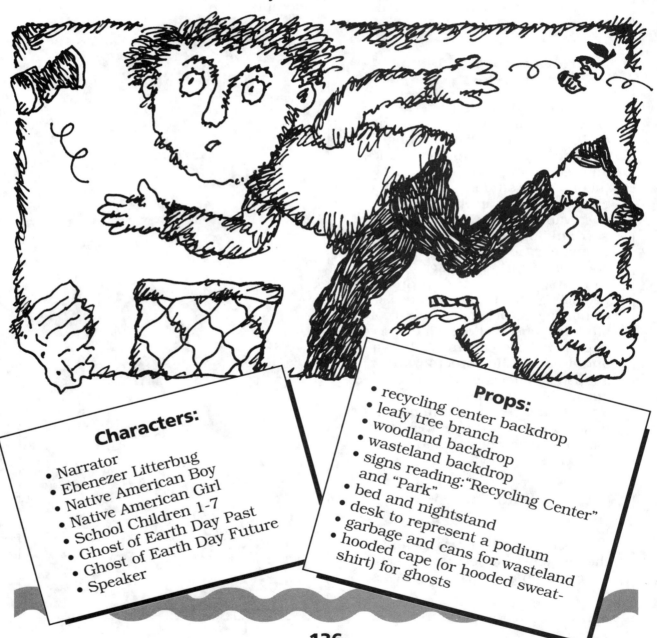

Characters:

- Narrator
- Ebenezer Litterbug
- Native American Boy
- Native American Girl
- School Children 1-7
- Ghost of Earth Day Past
- Ghost of Earth Day Future
- Speaker

Props:

- recycling center backdrop
- leafy tree branch
- woodland backdrop
- wasteland backdrop
- signs reading:"Recycling Center" and "Park"
- bed and nightstand
- desk to represent a podium
- garbage and cans for wasteland
- hooded cape (or hooded sweat-shirt) for ghosts

Production Note:

The stage should be set up so that a quarter of it is Ebenezer Litterbug's room with backdrops and props for the remainder of the stage varying for each act.

ACT 1

Outside of hometown America's Recycling Center.

Narrator: It was the day before Earth Day
And all through the town
No litter was anywhere,
Not uptown or down.

Ebenezer Litterbug: *[Walking outside of the recycling center kicking a can. Garbage is hanging out of his pocket.]* Bah, Earth Day!

Child 1: Hey! Ebenezer Litterbug! Tomorrow is Earth Day. The whole town has been cleaning for weeks. Pick up your garbage!

Ebenezer Litterbug: Mind your own beeswax! What do we pay street cleaners for?

Child 1: Looking after the environment is everybody's business, Ebenezer. That is what Earth Day is all about.

Ebenezer: Earth Day! Bah, Earth Day!

[Both children throw their hands up in frustration and they walk off in opposite directions.]

ACT 2

Ebenezer's bedroom, now located next to an American woodland scene as it was before the colonists arrived.

Narrator: Ebenezer Litterbug lay asleep in his bed
Sorry fellow, there was much to dread.

Ghost of Earth Day Past: *[Carrying a leafy tree branch to Ebenezer's bed, leans over and taps his shoulder.]* Rise and shine, Ebony baby!

Ebenezer: *[Sitting up with a start, rubbing his eyes.]* Who are you?

Ghost of Earth Day Past: I am the Ghost of Earth Day Past. You are making a mess of the Earth. You need a lesson. Come!

[Ebenezer gets out of bed and follows the Ghost to the woodland area.]

Ebenezer: Where are we? This is awesome, clean and green!

Ghost of Earth Day Past: We are in America in 1492. This is how our country looked before wasting and polluting became the ways of the land.

[Native American boy and girl walk past and stop in front of a tree.]

Native American Boy: Father says we must respect the Earth.

Native American Girl: If we treat her well she will reward us with food and all that is good.

[*Boy and girl walk offstage, skipping happily.*]

Ghost of Earth Day Past: All things here were pure and clean because the people took care of the Earth. We must leave now.

[*Ghost leads Ebenezer back to his bedroom.*]

Ghost of Earth Day Past: Wait for the next ghost. See you around Ebby!

Ebenezer: [*Waving.*] Bye!

[*Ebenezer lays down and the ghost walks offstage.*]

ACT 3

Ebenezer's bedroom which is now located next to the recycling center.

Narrator: Ebenezer was tossing and turning in bed.
          He wondered: "Where's the next ghost?
          What lies ahead?"

Ghost of Earth Day Present: [*Carrying a recycling sign, walks to Ebenezer's bed, leans over, and takes the covers off.*] Wake up sleepy head. We've got to make tracks out of here. [*He beckons with his finger to follow quickly to the recycling center.*]

Ebenezer: Who are you?

Ghost of Earth Day Present: I'm the Ghost of Earth Day Present. Follow me.

[*The two walk together to the recycling center.*]

Ebenezer: Why are we here?

Ghost of Earth Day Present: Look, listen, and learn.

[A group of children are standing by a podium where a speaker is talking.]

Speaker: The first Earth Day was on April 22, 1970. Earth Day is a day to enjoy our planet, learn about our planet, and help our planet. What can you do to help the Earth?

Child 2: Don't throw out your cans, glass, plastics, or papers. Recycle!

Child 3: Throw your garbage in a trash bin. Don't litter!

Child 4: Don't waste water. Fix leaky faucets. Turn the water off while you're brushing your teeth. Reduce water use!

Child 5: Walk, use the bus, or carpool. Energy is precious. Turn off lights and turn the heat down. Use it and we'll all lose it!

Child 6: Reuse your shopping bags, plastics, and aluminum foil. Always try to use things more than once.

Child 7: Recycle your toys, books, and clothes. Give them to children who need them.

Ebenezer: These kids really think that they can make a difference.

Ghost of Earth Day Present: *[While walking back to the bedroom.]* You had better hope so, Ebenezer. We are all depending on it. The next ghost will come to show you why.

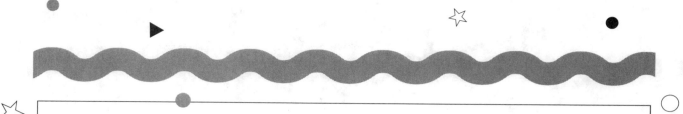

ACT 4

Ebenezer's bedroom, now next to a wasteland covered with garbage.

Narrator: Ebenezer waited,
Could he not guess?
He's about to see
One huge mess!!

[Ghost of Earth Day Future goes to Ebenezer's bed, taps his shoulder and walks away.]

Ebenezer: Hey, wait who are you? *[He jumps up and runs after the ghost to the vast wasteland, they stop to look around.]*

Ghost of Earth Day Future: I am the Ghost of Earth Day Future. I live here where there are no living things, only garbage and pollution.

Ebenezer: ARGHH!! This can't be! I'm out of here! *[Runs to hide under his blanket.]*

[Ghost exists.]

ACT 5

Ebenezer's bedroom; the town park and recycling center

Narrator: Ebenezer rose,
Not another thought in his head
It's Earth Day, by golly
I'm not staying in bed!

Ebenezer: *[Jumping up and running to the park to a group of children.]* Happy Earth Day, Everyone!

Child 1: Is that you Ebenezer Litterbug?

Ebenezer: Yes, it's me, but I've changed!

Child 2: Are you going to stop littering and polluting?

Ebenezer: Yes!

Child 3: Are you going to follow the three R's and always reuse, reduce, and recycle?

Ebenezer: Yes! Yes!

Child 4: Are you going to live in the spirit of Earth Day and take care of the world?

Ebenezer: Yes! Yes! Yes!

All: *[To the tune of "We Wish you a Merry Christmas"]*

> We wish you a Happy Earth Day,
> We wish you a Happy Earth Day,
> We wish you a Happy Earth Day,
> And Recycling Day, too!

> We will not waste or litter
> Wherever we go.
> We will help Mother Nature
> And we'll all live and grow!

> *[Repeat refrain.]*

The End

TEACHER'S GUIDE

An Earth Day Carol

Background

The first Earth Day was celebrated on April 22, 1970. Over the years, it has been commemorated in ways large and small. At the heart of any Earth Day effort is the knowledge that we must all work together to save our planet. Despite all of the gains since that first Earth Day, 200 million acres of tree cover have been lost and the population has grown by more than 1.6 billion (a figure equal to the world's population in 1900). Earth Day is recognized as being needed now more than ever. Some have suggested that it may become the biggest day of the year—a new "Green Christmas!"

Book Links

Brother Eagle, Sister Sky: A Message From Chief Seattle paintings by Susan Jeffers (Dial, 1991)

The River by David Bellamy (Potter, 1988)

The Salamander Room by Anne Mazer (Knopf, 1991)

Extension Activities

Environmental ABCs

Divide the class into small groups. Each group should write the alphabet, one letter per line. Then take a hike. You need not go far. Each group has to find something in nature that begins with each letter of the alphabet, then head back to the classroom to compare notes. You could use a graph to chart which letters had the largest number of different answers. Or you could vote on which item should represent each letter and create a nature alphabet for your classroom.

Green Newsletter

Do an environmental audit of your school. Compile a list of things that students and professionals are

already doing to help save the earth. Then make a list of actions that still need to be taken: Is litter being collected? Is there a lunchroom recycling program in place? Is noise pollution being controlled? Suggest that students work together to write up their findings and suggestions for future action. Compile their work into a environmental school newsletter and circulate the letter to all the classes. The letter should applaud all efforts to date, and challenge students to continue to do more.

Changes, Changes

Have students interview older adult family members to discover how their immediate environment was different when they were children. Develop a list of interview questions for the interviewees to answer, such as:

- Did they throw away as much garbage as we do now?

- What did they do with broken toys?

- How long did furniture last?

- How many pairs of shoes or how many articles of clothing did they own?

- What happened when children outgrew clothing?

- Can they tell of an area that was wild and is now built up with houses, stores, or other structures?

- How do they think the environment has changed over the years?

- What would they suggest to remedy any problems with the environment today?

Send a copy of the question list home with each child, along with directions asking the interviewee to answer the questions and fill in his/her name and area they lived as a child, as well as the time period during which he/she lived there. Have children share the results of the interviews in class. What kinds of environmental changes for the better or worse have occurred? What work needs to be done?

The Ugly Duckling

*A one-act pantomime play based on the story
by Hans Christian Andersen*

adapted by Mary Beth Spann

Characters:

- Narrator (adult or older student)
- Mother Duck
- Ugly Duckling
- Turkeys
- Old Woman
- Cat
- Man
- Children
- Ducklings
- Mr. Duck
- Wild Geese
- Hen
- Swans
- Chickens

Props/Costumes:

- white pillowcase costumes for Mother Duck, Mr. Duck, swans, and wild geese
- pillowcases dyed yellow for ducklings
- pillowcases dyed brown for the turkeys and the chickens

(continued on page 146)

145

Props/Costumes (continued):

- one case dyed gray for the Ugly Duckling (To prepare simple pillow case costumes, cut neck and arm holes in each case and slip them over children's heads. Fabric markers may then be used to draw feathers on the cases.)

- bird beak masks (created by opening the flaps in personal-size envelopes, punching holes in the ends of each envelope and threading a length of elastic thread through the holes. Flaps may be painted different colors to represent different bird beaks: orange for ducks; black for swans—including the Ugly Duckling; yellow for chickens and turkeys [with red paper waddle taped on turkey's beaks]; brown for wild geese. To wear a mask, a child slips the elastic behind the head and positions the beak mask in place over the bridge of the nose.)

- apron for Old Woman

- paper-covered cardboard box or laundry basket "nest"

- table and chair

Pantomime Production Notes:

The action words in italics in the following pantomime play suggest movements the students may act out. Before asking the children to pantomime any movements suggested by the story, have them listen as you read through the entire story line. Then print the underlined words on a piece of chart paper. As you familiarize students with the list, encourage them to suggest a variety of ways they might use movements to depict each action. Be prepared to offer some ideas of your own—especially for those movements that children may find difficult to envision. Jot any movement ideas in parenthesis next to the words on the list, for example:

pride turned to worry: puff-up chest, then press chest in and chew lip

tumbled: do somersault

waddled: walk stiff-legged with feet turned out

thought happily: lift eyes upwards with smile on face

struggling to keep up: waddle with baby steps

mocked: point, laugh, and rock back and forth from the waist

gliding: lean body to left and right

shuddered and shivered: shake shoulders as if cold

146

Narrator: Once upon a time in a barn there *sat* a mother duck warming the eggs in her nest. When the eggs began *hatching*, the mother duck was *proud* to see fluffy yellow ducklings *pecking* their way out of the eggshells. But the Mother Duck's *pride turned to worry* when she saw that the largest of the eggs had not yet hatched. "How strange!" *worried* the Mother Duck as her ducklings *quacked and pecked* about her feet. "That big egg doesn't look like my other eggs. I guess I'll have to sit on it a while longer." So she sat and she sat until finally, just when she *thought she could sit no more*, the egg *cracked open* and a very funny-looking gray bird *tumbled out*.

"Quack, quack!" *called* the mother duck as she *waddled* ahead of her new family. She *led* them down to the water into the pond where they all *swam and splashed about*. "I'm *happy to see* my funny-looking child can swim," she *thought happily* to herself.

"Quack, quack!" *called* the Mother Duck again as she *climbed* out of the pond and waddled back over to the barnyard with her children *struggling to keep up* behind her.

"What a good-looking family!" *clucked* the chickens as they *greeted* Mother Duck and her new children. But, Mr. Duck was not so kind to the new brood.

"What a funny-looking duckling," he *mocked* when he saw the big gray bird.

"Yes, he certainly is an ugly duckling," *gobbled* the mother turkey, bobbing her head back and forth. Then all the other chickens and ducks and turkeys began to *laugh and point* at the big bird. They *chased* him and tried to *peck* at him. Even the bird's brothers and sisters began to *peck* at him. Finally, the Ugly Duckling couldn't stand to be made fun of anymore, so, frightened and sad, he *flew up and away* over the barnyard gate and *landed* on the other side.

The Ugly Duckling *ran and ran* until he came to a marsh. There, he *sat down* to rest, but some wild geese *made fun* of him, *laughing and flapping their wings* in his face. So he ran away again.

The Ugly Duckling *ran and ran* until he saw a small cottage. He *slipped in* through the cottage door and there he *noticed* a little old woman *sitting and petting* her hen and her cat. The cat *asked* the Ugly Duckling if he could say "meow." The Ugly Duckling *shook his head* no. The hen *asked* the Ugly Duckling if he could lay eggs. The Ugly Duckling *shook his head* no. "Then you are of no use," *scolded* the old woman as she *shook her finger* at the Duckling.

"I'm of no use," thought the Ugly Duckling to himself, so he *hurried out* of the house and on to a nearby pond. It was while *gliding* on the pond that the duckling first *spotted* a flock of beautiful, big birds with long, graceful necks and strange, piercing cries. As the Duckling *watched*, the flock of birds *spread* their great wings, *lifted up* into the air, and *began flying* south for the winter. The Ugly Duckling hung his head low as he thought, "How I wish I could go with them. "Then he lifted his head and *cried out* the same piercing cry of the big birds.

When winter came, the Ugly Duckling *shuddered and shivered* in the freezing pond. A man *found* the bird and *carried* him home to be a pet for his family. But when the man's children tried to *chase after* the Ugly Duckling, the Ugly Duckling *grew frightened and* once again *flew away* into the cold night air. Winter lasted a long time, but finally spring *melted* the ice and snow. One day, the Ugly Duckling *spotted* some of the big, beautiful birds *flying* in the air. "How I wish I could swim with them!" thought the Ugly Duckling, so he *followed* the birds to the pond. When the Ugly Duckling *slipped* into the water, the big birds began to *swim* towards him. "They're going to peck me," he *worried* and he *bowed his head* to protect himself. But when the Ugly Duckling *looked down* and *caught sight* of his reflection in the water, he was *surprised* to see that he, too, was a big, beautiful white bird with a long, graceful neck! He was no longer ugly at all!

Then he noticed children at the pond's edge *throwing* the birds bread crumbs and *shouting* and waving. "Look!" they said,"The swans have come back! And, look at that new swan—he's the most beautiful of all!" Then the other swans *swam close and greeted* him by *stroking* him with their beaks. They *swam round* him and *bent down* before him as a sign of welcome.

The new swan felt so happy, he *stretched* his magnificent neck high and *spread* his glorious downy wings wide above the water. In his heart he finally realized that it didn't matter if he was born in a duck yard, since he came out of a swan's egg!

The End

TEACHER'S GUIDE

The Ugly Duckling

Background

Hans Christian Andersen is a sterling example of the power storytelling can have in one child's life. Born a cobbler's son on April 2, 1805 in Denmark, Hans loved to listen to his father read books aloud. He also relished the frequent times his grandmother would tell traditional folktales. Such rich, early experiences with literature fostered the storytelling and writing talents of this shy, imaginative child. The lasting legacy of such encounters can be found in the collections of Hans Christian Andersen's fairy tales and folktales we enjoy today.

Book Links

Hans Christian Andersen: The Complete Fairy Tales and Stories, translated from the Danish by Erik Chris Haugaard (Doubleday, 1984)

The Little Mermaid adapted by Anthea Bell (Picture Book Studio, 1984)

The Princess and the Pea interpreted by Paul Galdone (Seabury Press, 1978)

Extension Activities

Hans Christian Andersen Author Study

Secure a collection of Hans Christian Andersen stories to celebrate his birthday on April 2. (Children may be surprised to learn that some of their favorite tales, such as "The Little Mermaid," were written by Andersen.) Then create an author study graph by having children illustrate one favorite scene from each story you share. Label these illustrations with the story title and then post these illustrations in a horizontal line along the bottom of a bulletin board. Cut ice-skate shapes from white construction paper and label with the students' names. Glue silver glitter to the skate blades, if

desired. Then have children vote for their favorite story by posting their skates above the stories of their choice.

Appreciating Differences

Discuss the fact that in the end of the story, the Ugly Duckling really doesn't have a problem because, as it turns out, he has grown into a beautiful swan. Then ask them to imagine what if, as he grew, the Ugly Duckling remained a funny looking duck? What if people and other animals continued to make fun of him because he was different? How could the Ugly Duckling find happiness then?

Have students discuss how it feels to be called names and hurt because you look or behave differently. Invite them to talk of their own experiences, if they wish. Ask them to speculate what might motivate others to pick on the one who is different. Ask students to tell what the world would be like if we were all exactly the same. Round off your discussion by suggesting that students write or illustrate an alternative ending to the story line in which the Ugly Duckling remains different-looking, but learns positive ways to deal with others who hurt him.

Lift-the-Flap Bird Books

Have students research different types of birds and bird eggs, including the birds mentioned in the story. Invite students to draw pictures of their favorite birds' eggs on large pieces of removable sticky notes (one egg per note). Have students adhere each egg illustration to a piece of drawing paper. Students should then lift up each egg illustration and in the space on the drawing paper underneath, draw the picture of the corresponding bird that hatched from the egg. If desired, a written description of the egg can appear in the margin of drawing paper beneath the note, and the name of the bird can appear under the note, next to the bird illustration itself. Students can be helped to bind their bird egg collections together between construction paper covers titled "Lift-the-Flap Bird Books."

The Hidden Corn

A Folktale of the Mopan People of Mexico
adapted by Deborah Kovacs

Characters:

- Narrator
- Leaf Cutter Ant 1
- Leaf Cutter Ant 2
- Crow
- Woodpecker
- Yaluk: the Thunder Lord
- Coyote
- Boy
- Girl
- Skunk
- Fox

Props:

- a large rock
- white, red, yellow corn
- a bolt of lightning
- a red hat (for woodpecker to wear after lightning strikes)

ACT 1

Scene 1

Near a big rock in a forest.

Narrator: Once, long ago, people and animals did not eat corn. They ate fruit that grew on trees, and they ate roots that grew under the ground. Nobody had ever seen corn. But there was corn on earth—just one pile of kernels. It was under a rock in a big forest. One day, two ants crawled inside a tiny crack in the big rock. They found the corn.

Ant 1: Hey, this stuff is good!

Ant 2: Let's bring some to our nest.

Narrator: As the ants carried the corn kernels out from under the rock, they dropped one. A fox came along and ate it.

Fox: *[Crunching the corn kernel.]* That is the most delicious thing I ever put in my mouth.

Narrator: After that, every day, a whole army of leaf cutter ants came and took corn out from under the rock and took it back to their nest. And every day, the fox was waiting to pick up the kernels they dropped. Once, it started to rain. The ants dropped the kernels they were carrying, and ran for safety.

Fox: A whole pile of corn! Yippee!

Scene 2

Outside the fox's den.

Narrator: The fox had a feast. He ate so much corn that there was still some on his whiskers when he walked back to his den. Along the way, he ran into a crow, a skunk, and a coyote.

Crow: How's it going, Fox?

Fox: *[Still chewing.]* Mmm! Good!

Skunk: Say, what are you eating?

Fox: *[Still chewing, shakes his head.]* Oh, nothing.

Coyote: What's that on your whisker? *[Flicks corn off whiskers.]* Is this food? *[Tastes it.]* Say, that's mighty good! Where did you find it?

Fox: Oh, nowhere!

Scene 3

Back at the rock.

Narrator: The other animals were suspicious. They followed Fox the next day, and discovered his secret.

Coyote: So that's what he's up to.

Skunk: How do we get some?

Crow: Let's ask the ants for help.

Narrator: The ants did what they could. Again and again

they went into the crack, bringing out corn. Finally, they were worn out. The other animals wanted too much corn.

Ant 1: We can't help you any more.

Ant 2: Sorry.

Skunk: Let's try to squeeze into the crack. *[Tries, and fails.]*

Coyote: That's ridiculous!

Crow: Now what do we do?

Fox: Everything was okay until you guys butted in...

ACT 2

Scene 1

In a village.

Narrator: The animals asked a boy and a girl for help.

Boy: There's not much I can do. Wait! I have an Idea: I'll ask Yaluk, the Thunder God, for help.

Girl: He could send down a bolt of lightning to break the rock.

Scene 2

On a hill, above the village, overlooking the big rock. Children talking to Yaluk, who is higher on the hill than they are.

Narrator: The children called to Yaluk for help.

Boy/Girl: Yaluk! Please send down a lightning bolt to split this rock. We want to get the corn hidden inside.

Yaluk: Break a rock? That's a piece of cake. Fetch me a woodpecker, first.

Scene 3

In the forest.

Narrator: The boy and the girl searched the forest until they found a woodpecker.

Girl: Yaluk needs your help, Woodpecker!

Boy: Will you come with us?

Woodpecker: Yaluk? You mean *the* Yaluk? The Thunder God? Wow! You bet!

Scene 4

Outside the fox's den.

Yaluk: I want you to tap everywhere on that rock until you find the thinnest place.

Woodpecker: Yessir, Mr. Yaluk, sir! Right away! *[Woodpecker taps.]* Here's the spot you want!

Yaluk: Now stay back while I throw down this lightning bolt.

Narrator: The woodpecker tried to stay out of the way, but his curiosity got the better of him.

Woodpecker: I wonder what it looks like...

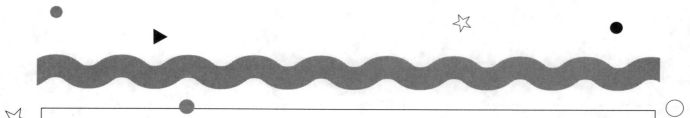

Narrator: The lightning bounced off the woodpecker's head.

Woodpecker: OUCH!

Boy: Are you all right?

Woodpecker: *[Dazed.]* I...I think so.

Girl: Your head feathers are all red!

Narrator: Yaluk split the rock open, and the boy and the girl took out corn to plant for their families, and to share with all the animals who wanted some. From that day to this, people and animals have eaten corn... *[Woodpecker wanders by, dazed.]*...And woodpeckers have always had red heads... *[To Woodpecker.]* Say, are you all right?

Woodpecker: I...I think so....

The End

TEACHER'S GUIDE

The Hidden Corn

Background

Mexico has been inhabited for more than 10,000 years. Until the 1500s, when Hernan Cortes conquered Mexico for Spain, Mexico was populated entirely by indigenous tribes, each with its own way of explaining the world. Myths and legends were an important way of conveying that information, and the myth-telling tradition has long been part of Mexican culture. "The Hidden Corn" is a familiar folktale that grows out of that condition. It is presented here in recognition of Cinco de Mayo, Mexico's annual Independence Day celebration.

Cinco de Mayo, Spanish for May 5, commemorates May 5, 1862, the day on which the decisive war against the final foreign power to invade Mexico, France, was begun.

Each year on May 5, celebrations of Mexican culture and traditions take place throughout Mexico and in many areas of the United States.

Book Links

The Mythology of Mexico and Central America by John Bierhorst (William Morrow and Company, 1990)

Tales from Jalisco by Howard T. Wheeler (American Folklore Society Publications, 1985)

Tales the People Tell in Mexico by Grant Lyons (Julian Messner, 1972)

Extension Activities

Introduction to Mexico

Have students locate Mexico on a map or globe. Ask if any of them have ever traveled to Mexico or if they own any Mexican products or artifacts. Have children imagine what life must be like in Mexico. Have them speculate about Mexico's climate, crops, animals, geography, and the dress, language, and life-styles of its people. Then research nonfiction books and

stories to discover what Mexico and her people are really like. Did students accurately describe Mexico and her people? How did your research affect how students regard Mexico and the people who live there?

Corn Fest

For thousands of years, corn has been a very important staple of the Mexican diet. Students can research this important food in a number of ways. Begin by providing samples of corn varieties and corn products such as fresh corn on the cob, frozen corn, canned corn, popcorn, cornmeal, corn bread, corn oil, corn muffins, corn chips, etc. Ask students to tell what they know about these products. Ask them to tell what they know about how it grows and how corn is used to make baked goods. As you talk together, develop a list of corn vocabulary children may incorporate into their creative writing and research reports. As a follow-up to this introduction, students can research the role of corn in the Mexican diet. They can also collect recipes for Mexican dishes that incorporate corn, and learn about the nutritional value of corn.

An Origin-al Idea

"The Hidden Corn" is an example of an origin story, a story devised to explain the origin of a certain aspect of life. Students can do research to learn about more Mexican origin stories and may learn about origin stories from different cultures. With their research complete, have students select one origin story to depict on a mural. Have students make a list of what in the story happened first, second, third, etc. Then divide a bulletin board into enough vertical panels to represent each sequential event in the story. Have students fill in each panel with words and illustrations so as to retell the story.

Becoming a Butterfly

by Tara McCarthy

Props:

- several very large green construction paper leaves
- a folding screen, behind which Stripes, will eventually hide from the audience.
- a green-yellow ball (paint or wrap with green papier mâché) to repesent the butterfly egg
- lengths of green crepe paper for Stripe's pupa costume
- three pairs of colorful wings: one pair for Madame Butterfly; the second pair eventually for Stripes; the third pair for Wiggles. (Wings can be cut from tag board, then painted. Affix to clothing with double faced masking tape.)

Characters:

- Fred Frog
- Phoebe, Robin, and Jay: birds
- Madame Butterfly
- Stripes: a caterpillar on the way to becoming a butterfly
- Wiggles: another caterpillar

160

ACT 1

A warm day in early spring. The egg is lying on the leaves. Fred is sitting next to it.

Fred: Harumph! Harumph! Every spring I find a whole lot of these eggs. Madame Butterfly just plops them on leaves and flies away! Now I ask you, what kind of parenting is that?

[The birds come flying in and heads for the egg.]

Phoebe: Hey, look guys! What a yummy morsel to eat!

Jay: Let me at it! I'm starving!

Fred: Hold on there! This is one egg you're *not* going to eat. Not while ol' Fred's here to stand guard!

Robin: Oh, come on, Fred! It's just an *egg!*

Fred: Harumph! Harumph! A lot *you* know! In a very short while, this egg is going to be a caterpillar. *[Stripes crawls on stage and starts to nibble a leaf.]* Just like that caterpillar over there!

Phoebe: Even better! Caterpillars are even tastier than eggs. *[She heads for Stripes; Stripes looks up, scared.]*

Fred: Phoebe! Keep your beak off that caterpillar! In a few days, that caterpillar is going to be a pupa. Now you go right on eating, Stripes. I'll take care of you. *[Stripes continues nibbling.]*

Jay: Egg, caterpillar, pupa! Whatever are you croaking on about, Fred?

Robin: A thing by any other name tastes just as good, Fred!

Fred: Well *this* thing is a surprising thing! And you're in for the surprise of your life, because the pupa is going to be a BUTTERFLY!

[The birds all burst into laughter.]

Phoebe: A butterfly! You've gotta be kidding! *[Madame Butterfly comes flying in. She is humming a little tune.]* You mean that wiggly, ugly little crawly blob is going to be a gorgeous creature like that?

Madame Butterfly: Oh, yes, indeed. This *[pointing to the egg]* is my youngest child, and this *[pointing to Stripes]* is my eldest. I started off life in the very same way.

Fred: Harumph! Well, you might stick around and help me guard these kids of yours!

Madame Butterfly: I can't stick around. I have to collect nectar. It's what I eat, you know. *[She flies away.]*

Jay: *[Grumbling.]* Well, we're going to stick around, because we don't believe a word of any of this! Egg, caterpillar, pupa, butterfly. What a lot of nonsense!

ACT 2

A few days later. The egg is gone, and Wiggles has taken its place. Wiggles is nibbling a leaf. To the side of the stage, Stripes is winding green crepe paper around himself from head to toe. The birds are staring in amazement.

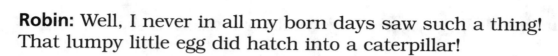

Robin: Well, I never in all my born days saw such a thing! That lumpy little egg did hatch into a caterpillar!

Fred: Harumph! Stick with me, and you'll learn a lot, kiddo!

Phoebe: Look at Stripes! He's turning all green and shiny!

Fred: I told you that was going to happen. Stripes is becoming a pupa. *[Stripes shuffles off to hide behind the screen. His wings are hidden behind it.]*

Jay: He's gone! We'll never see him again!

Wiggles: Where's my brother going?

Fred: Don't worry! He's going to find a nice quiet leaf to hang onto for a week or so. Probably wants to get away from all you noisy birds!

Robin: What a terrible fate! From a nice little crawly thing with legs to a quiet little blob...I mean pupa...hanging very still.

[From behind the screen, Stripes is making little surprised noises. These continue softly while the other characters talk.]

Stripes: Ooh...ahh...wow...look at that...hmm!...what next?...ouch...whee!...it's dark in here!...not too roomy!...

Fred: Harumph! Inside that little pupa, a lot is happening. Stripes the Caterpillar is turning into a butterfly.

Wiggles: That's going to happen to me, too! My mama says that when *I'm* a pupa, parts of my body will change into whole different parts. Only my inside parts will stay the same.

Phoebe: Well, guys, shall we wait for a week to see the final act?

Robin and Jay: We wouldn't miss it for the world!

ACT 3

A week later. The birds and Fred are staring in the direction of the screen. Wiggles has disappeared. Another egg is on the leaves.

Stripes: *[From behind the screen.]* Finished! Done! Look out, world, here I come!

Fred: Get ready for a beautiful surprise!

[Stripes comes out from behind the screen, moving and fluttering his wings. The birds flop onto the floor in amazement.]

Birds: Wow!...Fantastic!...the greatest!...

Stripes: I agree! Now I'm off to gather nectar. *[He flies away.]*

Jay: No, come back, come back!

Robin: He didn't even say good-bye to his brother!

Phoebe: Where is Wiggles, anyway? Oh, my! *[She points at the egg.]* Wiggles turned back into an egg!

Fred: Harumph! Don't be silly! You know that's not the way it happens!

Jay: Yes, don't be silly, Phoebe! That's not Wiggles. But that egg will become a caterpillar, too...

164

Robin: ...and the caterpillar will become a pupa, and...

Wiggles: *[From offstage.]* That's me, folks! I'm a pupa today, but by and by....

Fred and Birds: You're going to be a butterfly!

[Wiggles flutters out as everyone applauds.]

The End

TEACHER'S GUIDE

Becoming a Butterfly

Background

There are anywhere from 15,000 to 20,000 species of butterflies in the world, which scientists have grouped into families, according to the physical features these insects have in common. Among the chief families are nine that frequent North America. Your students may have seen members of the skipper family; of the blues, coppers, and hair streaks family; of the satyrs and wood nymphs family. And among the milkweed family is the beautiful monarch butterfly, a familiar visitor wherever milkweed still stands, and probably the one that first comes to mind when children hear the word *butterfly*.

Every butterfly goes through four stages of development, called *metamorphosis*. The egg is deposit-ed on a leaf that will provide food for the caterpillar, or larva, that will emerge. After eating enough to grow to its full size, the caterpillar becomes a pupa by attaching itself to a sheltered, high spot, depositing a sticky liquid to fasten itself there, and forming a hard shell. Inside this shell, the larval structures are reshaped into those of a butterfly. About an hour after the butterfly emerges from this shell, it is ready to fly. The length of the pupa stage varies. For some species, it lasts more than a year, for others a few weeks or a few days.

Book Links

Bugs: Poems by Mary Ann Hoberman (Viking, 1976)

If At First You Do Not See by Ruth Brown (Henry Holt, 1983)

The Very Hungry Caterpillar by Eric Carle (Putnam, 1981)

Extension Activities

But Is It a Butterfly?

Invite students to form two groups and find out about the dif-

ferences between moths and butterflies. Offer children construction-paper moths and butterflies to decorate with markings to record fast facts. Groups can display their shapes on a bulletin board. Since most butterflies are active during the day and most moths are active at night, you might divide the board in half, the butterfly half covered with yellow paper representing day, and the moth half covered with black representing night.

Parents and Their Offspring

Many living things have first-forms that hardly resemble their parents at all. (As an example, you might discuss the fact that Fred, the frog began life as a polliwog.) If you have an opportunity to do so, take your class to a brook in springtime where they can observe both the polliwogs and their parents. Look in animal resource books to discover more examples of baby animals that do and do not resemble their parents at birth. Invite children to paint pictures of parents and babies on a mural.

That's a Long Trip!

Invite a group of students to research the migration of Monarch butterflies. Provide a large outline map of North America on which they can draw the routes the butterflies take and note the times of year when these migrations take place. Students can add illustra-tions to the map to show the butterflies themselves, the places where their eggs are laid, and the milkweed plants the larvae and adults use for food. Ask them to calculate the mileage covered by the migrating butterflies on both legs of their fantastic voyage.

A Kindness Returned

by Robin Bernard

Characters:
- Narrator
- Mom
- Dad
- Stephie
- Pam
- Adam

Props:
- kitchen backdrop
- table and chairs
- cartons, dishes
- telephone
- toy cat (realistic)
- books
- lunch boxes

ACT 1

Kitchen of the Williams's home, winter.

Narrator: The Williams have just moved from an apartment into a house. Although moving was a big job, the family is happy to be in their new home and are busy unpacking.

[The kitchen door opens and Pam comes in carrying something inside her jacket.]

Pam: Look, everybody! Look what I found near the garbage cans! Poor kitty, she's so *skinny*! Can we keep her, Mom? Can we, Dad?

Dad: Well...

Stephie: *[Rushing to look.]* She's *cold* and *wet*!

Adam: *[Rushing to look.]* She must be *starving*!

Pam: And she has no collar!

Children: *Please*, can we keep her?

Mom: We'll see. But first *[looking at the cat in Pam's arms]* we better get her warm and fed. Here's a towel, Pam. You dry her off while I heat up a saucer of milk.

Stephie: *[Looking in the refrigerator.]* I'll find something for her to eat.

Adam: *[Grabbing an empty carton.]* I'll make a bed for her!

Dad: *[Picking up the telephone.]* And I better call the police and pound to see if anybody has reported losing a cat.

ACT 2

Two weeks later. The family is at the kitchen table eating dinner.

Stephie: *[Looking into the cat's bed.]* Cleo looks so good, Mom: She must like your cooking! Her coat is shiny, and she's not skinny anymore.

Pam: Listen to her purr. She's so happy here!

Adam: *[Speaking to his father.]* We *are* going to keep her, Dad, aren't we?

Dad: Probably Adam, but we can't be sure for another few days. If nobody answers the ad we put in the newspaper, Cleo will officially belong to us.

[As Pam gets up to put her plate in the sink, the telephone rings. She answers it.]

Pam: *[Dropping the phone receiver and running out of the room crying.]* No! It's not fair! Cleo is OUR cat!

[Stephie and Adam hurry after Pam.]

ACT 3

Later, the same night.

Adam: But I don't *want* to give Cleo away! How do we know they'll take good care of her?

Stephie: How do we know they'll feed her enough?

Pam: How do we know they'll love her as much as we do?

Mom: All of you—just listen. The Nelsons moved here just a week before we did and Muffin—our Cleo—got lost the very first day. That's why she was so skinny when Pam found her. And their little girl has been crying ever since because she misses her cat so much. Just try to imagine how she feels.

Pam: We don't have to imagine, Mom. We'll feel just as bad when they come to take her back.

Dad: I know it hurts to give up Cleo, but she belongs to the Nelsons. They've been worried sick about her, and were afraid they might never see her again. We have to give Cleo back to her family; that's where she belongs.

[The children sadly nod their heads and leave the room looking thoroughly miserable.]

ACT 4

Two months later. Mrs. Williams is looking out of the kitchen window. The children come in carrying their school books and lunch boxes.

Mom: Don't take your coats off, kids. We have a party to go to.

Adam: A party?

Stephie: Whose party?

Pam: Is it a birthday party?

Mom: Yes—and it's for *triplets*!

Children: *Triplets*!?

Mom: Well, furry triplets. Mrs. Nelson called this morning to thank all of you. She said if you hadn't taken such good care of Muffin, she never would have had such healthy kittens!

Children: *Kittens*!?

Mom: Three of them...six weeks old today, and there's one for each of you!

[The children laugh and cheer, and rush out the door with their mother.]

The End

TEACHER'S GUIDE

A Kindness Returned

Background

The first seven days of May are set aside for a very special event: Be Kind to Animal Week! From guppies to Great Danes, tarantulas to tabbies, all sorts of pets are known to have a positive effect on people of all ages. As loving companions, built-in alarm systems, and antidotes for boredom and even depression, they can be demanding, heroic, mysterious, and comical. Mostly, they absorb our affection and return it tenfold.

Book Links

Be Kind to Animals by James Duffy (Western Publishers, 1988)

Pet Show by Ezra Jack Keats (Macmillan, 1972)

That Dog by Nanette Newman (Thomas Y. Crowell, 1983)

Extension Activities

The Best Pets

Share the following chant with your students:

CHORUS:
If I had a pet, pet, pet,
Which one would I get, get, get?
If I had a pet, pet, pet,
To care for and to play with.

For a puppy of my own,
I would find a juicy bone.
Walk my puppy every day,
Teach it how to fetch and stay!

REPEAT CHORUS

For a kitten I would bring
A playful little ball of string.
Pour some milk into a cup,
Watch my kitty lap it up.

REPEAT CHORUS

For a fish I'd have a tank,
Making sure it ate and drank.
Feed it daily once or twice,
Change the water, keep it nice!

REPEAT CHORUS

For a bird I'd bring some seed,
And a cage the bird would need.
Listen as it chirped its song,
Sing out birdie, all day long!

REPEAT CHORUS
—by Meish Goldish

After you've read and enjoyed the poem, invite students to share their thoughts about what animals they think make the best pets. Children should each pick a favorite pet and generate a list describing the pet's attributes. Then ask children to use their list to write advertisements "selling" their classmates on their pets. As a variation, children can try selling classmates on unlikely pet choices (such as wild animals, underwater animals, etc.). Remind children that while owning wild animals is not a good idea, it is OK to imagine it.

Pet Graph

Help children chart the number and kinds of pets they own. First, make a list of students' pets (fish, dogs, cats, etc.). Then ask each student to name the number and kind of pets he or she has (or has ever had). Enter the information onto the chart. Also, add other descriptive animal criteria to your chart such as feathers, fur, two feet, four feet, beak, claws, etc. Have children use the chart to check off the criteria that applies to their animals.

Pin-up Pet Poster

Ask students to bring in photos of their pets. (Those with no pets can bring in magazine photos of pets they'd like to have some day). Have the children paste their pictures collage-style onto on a large sheet of posterboard. Use the poster to play a pet guessing game. Make up game questions such as:

- How many legs are there on the poster?
- How many mammals (or reptiles or amphibians) are on the poster?
- How many animals on the poster begin with the letter A (or B, or C, etc.)?

Betsy Ross, Seamstress with a Mission

by Eve Spencer

Characters:

- Narrator
- Betsy Ross
- Grandchildren 1-4
- George Washington
- George Ross
- Robert Morris
- Murmuring Crowd

Props:

- colonial-style clothing for Betsy Ross, Washington, George Ross, and Robert Morris
- shirt with ruffles
- desk and chairs
- scissors
- paper prefolded into a star
- pencil
- two large flag drawings: Washington's original sketch and the revised sketch (see page 182)

ACT 1

Philadelphia, Pennsylvania, 1825, at the home of Betsy Ross.

Narrator: Betsy Ross was born in 1752 and lived most of her life in the city of Philadelphia. She was an excellent seamstress and owned a sewing and upholstery shop for many years. Betsy Ross mostly is remembered for the sewing of our nation's first flag. It is a story that Betsy herself liked to tell her children and grandchildren.

Grandchild 1: Tell us a story, Grandma Betsy.

Grandchild 2: Yes, Grandma, a story!

Betsy: Certainly! What story would you like to hear?

Grandchild 3: Tell the story about the flag—

Grandchild 4: And the day you met George Washington!

Betsy: Ah, yes. That was an extraordinary day. An extraordinary time, really. It was the time when our country was newly born and fighting to survive.

Grandchild 2: When was that, Grandma?

Betsy: Well, let's see. It was almost 50 years ago, in 1776. I was 24 years old then. My husband John had recently died in an accident.

Grandchild 1: You must have been really sad, Grandma.

Betsy: Oh, I was terribly sad.

Grandchild 3: And you had to run your sewing shop all by yourself, didn't you?

Betsy: That's right, darling. I was trying very hard to keep my business open. But work was slow. The war against England was being fought, you know. I was worried I might have to close the shop. Until one day that spring, when my uncle, Congressman George Ross, came into my shop…

ACT 2

May 1776, inside Betsy's sewing shop in Philadelphia.

Betsy: *[Sitting and speaking to herself.]* Hmmm…These shirt ruffles are tricky to make…*[Hears noise, looks up]*…What's that commotion outside?

Murmuring Crowd: It's him! It's him! It's General Washington!

[Enter George Ross, George Washington, and Robert Morris.]

George Ross: Good afternoon, Betsy.

Betsy: Why Uncle, hello!

George Ross: Betsy, I'd like to introduce General George Washington from Virginia, the commander-in-chief of our continental army, and Robert Morris, my fellow Pennsylvania congressman.

Betsy: *[Somewhat flustered.]* Oh, my! Well, it's a great, great honor, sir, to meet you, General Washington, sir, and you, Congressman Morris.

George Washington: Pleased to meet you, Mrs. Ross.

Robert Morris: How do you do, Mrs. Ross?

George Washington: Mrs. Ross, I was terribly sorry to hear about the death of your husband. I know times must be hard for you right now. But we have a great favor to ask. And it must be kept secret!

Betsy: A secret? Well, I can certainly keep a secret.

George Washington: Good! Your uncle told me you were trustworthy. He also said you were the best seamstress in Philadelphia. So that's why we want you to make a flag.

Betsy: A flag?

George Washington: Yes, Mrs. Ross, a flag! Our thirteen colonies have joined forces to fight a war for independence. Together we'll win the war, and together we'll form a new nation. And our new nation needs a symbol—a flag—to bring all of us together as Americans. Will you make it?

Betsy: I'm very honored to be asked, sir. But I don't know if I can—

Robert Morris: Don't worry about the money, Mrs. Ross. We'll give you all you need.

Betsy: Oh, it's not the money, sir. It's just that I've never made a flag before. But if you wish, I...I can try.

George Washington: Good! Now take a look at this sketch I made. *[He pulls out sketch of flag and posts it on wall.]* What do you think?

Betsy: *[Looking thoughtfully at the sketch.]* Oh, that's a lovely flag, General, sir. It's very...square.

George Washington: Well, yes. Most flags are square, Mrs. Ross.

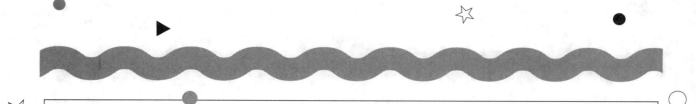

Betsy: *[Shyly.]* Yes, I guess they are. But take a look at these stripes, General. Maybe they'd seem bolder and brighter if they were longer?

George Ross: Betsy, I'm sure the General doesn't want to hear…

George Washington: No, she has an interesting point. Longer stripes would look better.

Betsy: I like the idea of having 13 stars and 13 Stripes.

George Washington: Yes, I thought that would be nice. You know, one star and one stripe for each of the 13 colonies.

Betsy: But what about these stars, General? Do you think they would look nicer if they were arranged in a shape? I don't know—maybe something round?

George Washington: Hmmm. Maybe the stars should be in a circle. Yes, that might work!

Betsy: *[Emboldened.]* And what if the stars had five points instead of six? I think five-pointed stars look better.

George Washington: I think so, too. But aren't five-pointed stars hard to make?

Betsy: Actually, General, a five-pointed star is very easy to make.

George Washington: It is?

Betsy: Oh, yes. Here, let me show you. *[She takes a piece of paper, folds it.]* Now watch. I'll make just *one snip* with the scissors…*[She makes a cut.]* Now look! *[She unfolds the* *paper to show a perfect five pointed star.]*

George Washington: Amazing!

Robert Morris: Just *one* snip!

George Ross: Betsy, that's very nice, but I'm sure the General has given a lot of thought to his design.

George Washington: Well, actually, I've been very busy lately. And your niece has made some good suggestions. Let me see if I can make a new sketch using her ideas. *[Sits down at desk and redraws the flag, then holds up the new sketch.]* What do you think?

Betsy: Perfect!

George Washington: Then this will be the flag you'll make.

Betsy: I'll get started right away.

George Washington: Excellent! I must say it's been a real pleasure meeting you, Mrs. Ross. Your suggestions were a great inspiration. Thank you.

Betsy: *[Greatly pleased.]* Why, thank *you*, sir!

[The three men say good-bye and leave.]

Narrator: Immediately after the men left her shop, Betsy started working on the flag. She bought the materials she needed and even borrowed a flag to study how it was made. And in a very short while, the flag was completed and approved. George Washington and the others liked it so much that Betsy received a contract to continue making flags for the government.

ACT 3

Philadelphia, Pennsylvania, 1825, at the home of Betsy Ross.

Betsy: And that was the beginning of my flag-making business!

Grandchild 4: Grandma, why was the flag a secret?

Betsy: Well, dear, those were dangerous times. We were at war. It would have been terrible if the English had known about it.

Grandchild 2: Are you a hero, Grandma?

Betsy: Well, dear, I've heard some say that's so. But I feel I was just doing my duty.

Grandchild 1: Grandma, that's a great story. I'm going to tell it to my own children and grandchildren some day.

Betsy: That would be wonderful, darling. But promise me something, all of you. Promise me that one day you will all be something special in your own lives. It doesn't have to be something big, just something meaningful. And then you'll have your very own stories to tell your grandchildren. Will you try to do that?

All: We will!

Betsy: Good. Now, it's getting late, so let's say goodnight.

All: Goodnight!

The End

TEACHER'S GUIDE

Betsy Ross, Seamstress with a Mission

Background

Flag Day is celebrated on June 14th in commemoration of the day the Continental Congress adopted the nation's first flag. Was this the flag that Betsy Ross made? Most historians say no, because her claim cannot be verified. Still, the story persists as a legend. It was first brought to the nation's attention by Betsy Ross's grandson, William Canby, who remembered hearing the family story from his Aunt Clarissa, Betsy's daughter. Canby presented the charming flag story to the Historical Society of Pennsylvania in 1870. The story later appeared in *Harper's* magazine, and was soon being taught to school children across the country. Although William Canby tried to document his grandmother's story, he could never find any proof. However, there's no doubt that Betsy Ross was a real person. She was born Betsy Griscom in Philadelphia in 1752 and grew up in a large, supportive household. Betsy was a gifted seamstress and worked as an apprentice at an upholsterer's shop, where she met John Ross. They later married and opened a shop of their own.

Washington's original sketch

Ross' revised sketch

Book Links

A Flag for Our Country by Eve Spencer (Steck-Vaughn Company, 1993)

Betsy Ross: Designer of Our Flag by Ann Weil (Aladdin Books, 1986)

Extension Activities

Family Stories

The legend of Betsy Ross and the first flag began as a family story. Talk with students about family stories—how they're shared orally among family members, retold many times, and often passed from one generation to the next. Also talk about some common sources for these stories, such as a journey from a foreign homeland to the United States, a relative's efforts during a war, and unusual acts of bravery, kindness—or even silliness! Then invite students to tell stories about their own families. Either on their own or with a partner, students can brainstorm ideas and choose a family story they want to share orally with a small group. Students might also enjoy writing down and illustrating their stories with drawings or photographs to include in a class Family Album.

All Stars

There really is a way to make a five-pointed star with just one snip!

Demonstrate this method for students and invite them to try it using blunt-edged scissors.

1. Fold a square piece of paper in half.
2. Fold corner D to a point midway between A and C.
3. Fold corner C up.
4. Fold corner X over to F Cut along dotted line.

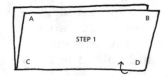

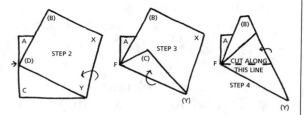

(Note: To avoid any mistakes during a play performance, have players use a precut star, or a prefolded star with a dotted line.)

Star Math

Here are two fun ways to use the stars.

• Have cooperative groups make sets of seven stars. For variety, students can use colored or textured paper. Challenge each group to arrange the stars in as many patterns as possible.

Groups can then tape their favorite star designs to posterboard or mural paper. Students may also want to try creating designs with 13 stars—the same number as in Betsy's flag. Use this activity to help develop students' sense of spatial relationships.

• Invite each student to write a number problem, a word problem, a fortune, or a riddle on a star. They can then fold up their stars and place them in a large communal box. Have each student then draw a star from the box, unfold it, and solve the problem or read the fortune or riddle aloud. Display completed stars on a bulletin board.

Flag Day

Prepare for a celebration of Flag Day on June 14 with these suggestions.

• Challenge students to make a flag for your class or school. Team up pairs of students to work together cooperatively, just as Betsy Ross and George Washington did to design the first Stars and Stripes!

• Betsy Ross didn't keep a journal, but what if she had? What would she have recorded on that day in May, 1776, when she met George Washington? Encourage students to write imaginary entries for Betsy's diary.

• Have groups of students brainstorm ideas for a commemorative song or poem honoring Betsy Ross and her flag.

• Write or call the Betsy Ross House in Philadelphia, Pennsylvania, for more information about the life and times of Betsy Ross:

Betsy Ross House
239 Arch Street
Philadelphia, PA 19106
(215) 627-5343

Summer Dreams

by James Halverson

Characters:

- Narrator
- Three classmates: Maria, Christopher, and Lou
- TV set (2 Students)
- Bed (1 or 2 students)
- Ghost of the School Year

Props:

- spray bottle filled with water
- rope or heavy twine
- small bed sheet
- pillow (optional)
- several books

ACT 1

Maria, Christopher, and Lou walking home from school.

Narrator: Dreams of summer,
Dreams of play,
Dreams that school will go away.
Maria, Christopher, and Lou
Dream of what they're going to do
Once the long school year is through.

Maria: I can't *wait* for the end of school!

Christopher: I know! No more reading, no more spelling!

Lou: No more subtraction!

Maria: It's going to be wonderful. I'm not going to do anything except watch TV!

Christopher: I'm just going to play with my friends. I won't
read a thing.

Lou: What I dream about is staying up as late as I want.

Maria: Nothing but TV and more TV!

Lou: It will be great. No school in the morning. I'll *never* go
to bed!

Christopher: And no one will make me read a book!

*[During this last speech the Ghost of the School Year sneaks
onto the stage and sprays each of them with a magical spray
gun. The moment the mist covers them, they fall into a happy
dream of the future.]*

Ghost: Let them hope.
Let them dream.
Things may not be
As they seem.
I'm a wicked little haunt:
I'm going to give them what they want!
When they wake, they're going to see
The summer that they wished to be.

ACT 2

Narrator: What was it that Maria wished for?
TV shows: "More! Give me more!"

[Two students move onto the stage holding hands in such a way as to make the rectangular shape of a TV screen. Attached to them by a rope is Maria, who is dragged onto the stage as if she were a prisoner.]

TV: Happy to have you with us today, Maria: This is your treat:
Lots of stuff,
Lots of stuff—
Time for a commercial—
Same old stuff!

Maria: Help! I've seen this all before. I'll change the channel.

[She twists an imaginary dial or points a remote control at the TV.]

TV: Happy to have you with us today, Maria. This is your treat:

Lots of stuff.
Lots of stuff.
Time for a commercial—
Same old stuff!

Maria: You said that before. You're boring. I didn't really mean that I *only* wanted to watch TV: I mean, I did like lots of the things at school—

TV: School? School?
  That's the word that rhymes with *fool!*

[TV leads Maria offstage.]

[They exit.]

Narrator: Lou, you remember, clearly said
  He'd never ever go to bed!

[Two children representing Lou's bed enter. They are holding a small sheet between them and, perhaps a pillow. Lou staggers onstage, yawning and exhausted, and tries to get into bed. Every time he tries to lie down, the bed evades him or dumps him to the floor.]

Lou: I'm so sleepy…I just want to go to bed…Ouch, why can't I get into this thing? Oh, why did I ever wish such a silly wish?

[The bed leads him offstage as he continues to try to lie down and rest.]

Narrator: Now let's see how Christopher looks.
  He's the one who swore off books.

[A bookcase enters—one or two students holding out books

stiffly as if they were a shelf. Christopher enters soon after, angrily stamping his feet.]

Christopher: That's the last time I play with my brother! We always argue about what game to play. Then when we finally do get around to playing, he always tries to boss me around. I need some time to myself.

[The bookcase moves towards him in a teasing way.]

Christopher: I know I said I wouldn't want to read. But if I do, no one at school will ever know.

[He reaches for a book, but it moves out of reach. As he tries again, one of the other books gives him a cuff on the shoulder.]

Christopher: What's going on? Why can't I read? These books are acting just like my brother! I thought at least books would still be my friends. I wish I were back in school!

[The bookcase leads him off stage as he tries unsuccessfully to read.]

ACT 3

The three classmates are onstage in just the same positions as when they were originally squirted by the ghost.

Narrator: Maria, Christopher, and Lou,
Have seen their summer dreams come true.

[The Ghost of the School Year enters, squirts them again, and they awaken.]

Maria: Oh, I'm still here in school. I had the worst… I don't know what to call it. I hope it was just a dream!

Christopher: I dreamed that I really couldn't read all summer.

Lou: And I couldn't ever go to bed. I was so tired! It wasn't fun at all.

Maria: Watching TV all the time was like being in prison.

Christopher: Maybe vacation isn't going to be just what we thought.

Maria: And maybe school is OK.

Lou: I'm still going to have fun on vacation. But, you know, I'll probably look forward to coming back to school next fall, too.

[Enter Ghost of the School Year unseen behind them.]

Ghost: I'm going to teach them a little poem:
 Summer's OK, school's OK,
 Neither of them is here to stay.
 In summer we go different ways,
 But we'll be back another day,
 And we'll put on another play!

Maria: Summer's OK, school's OK—

Christopher: Neither of them is here to stay—

Lou: In summer we go different ways—

All: But we'll be back another day—
        And we'll put on another play.

*[The entire cast comes on stage and together chants the
Ghost's poem.]*

The End

TEACHER'S GUIDE

Summer Dreams

Background

Summer can be a glorious time for children to look forward to, but it also is a time that can signal uncertainty and change. After all, the freedom of summer brings an end to some comfortable home-away-from-home routines that were created during an entire school year. It means saying good-bye to a familiar past and hello to an uncertain future. For many children, the beginning of summer is a bittersweet time of letting go and moving on. For teachers, the awareness that children may be struggling inside can go a long way toward helping them make a smooth and happy transition out of the classroom and into the sunshine.

Book Links

Bigmama's by Donald Crews (Greenwillow Books, 1991)

The Goodbye Book by Judith Viorst (Macmillan, 1988)

Magic Beach by Alison Lester (Little Brown and Co., 1992)

Up and Down on the Merry-Go-Round by Bill Martin, Jr. and John Archambault (Henry Holt and Co., 1985 and 1988)

Extension Activities

See How We've Grown!

Students of any age benefit from seeing how far they've come and noting all they've accomplished during the school year. To this end, you can easily use your planbook as the basis for helping to create a class field trip down memory lane. Before school comes to a close, set aside time to go back through the pages of your lesson plans and make a list of all the learning experiences you shared together. For example, you might include any theme units you covered, all the songs you learned, poems you enjoyed and all the skills students mastered together. In addition, pull out some of your class photos, including pictures of displays and projects the children worked on throughout the year. Then set aside time for a "remember when..." session. Present your memories and memorabilia and then invite students to add some of their own best memories to the mix. Finish off by having children each write and illustrate one page for a class book titled "Our Class Memories." Make photocopies of each page— plus a blank page simply titled "Autographs" so that each child can own a copy of the book for classmates to sign.

Mysterious Sunshine Riddles

Invite children to bring in one item that reminds them of summer. Place the items into a large cardboard mystery box you've decorated with glued-on summer symbols (sun, sand, pail, and shovel, sunglasses, etc.) cut from construction paper or craft paper. Have students take turns offering clues describing their summery items for the other students to guess. If you wish, you can turn their descriptions into instant Summer Mystery Riddles by copying down the words each student uses and then finishing up with the name of the item being described. For example:

A Summer Riddle
It's silver.

It has a wooden handle.
Mom uses it for cookouts.
It's a *spatula!*

A Summer Riddle
I wear it.
It stretches.
It's purple.
I can get it wet.
It's a *bathing suit!*

Booking the Summer

Remind students of all the reading you've done together by compiling a list of the titles of books and stories you've shared as a class. Then offer children a suggested summer reading list that builds on the foundation you've laid all year long. For example, if in class students enjoyed a particular author, cite other books by that same author. If children read one of a series of books, recommend that they continue reading the rest of the titles. And, finally, if students enjoyed a book that is available on film, suggest that they reread the book and enjoy viewing the story on some rainy summer day with their families.

193

NOTES

NOTES

NOTES

NOTES

NOTES

NOTES

NOTES